Studies in Earliest Christianity

Robert L. Greenhow

WESTBOW·
PRESS
A DIVISION OF THOMAS NELSON
& ZONDERVAN

WestBow Press books may be ordered through booksellers or by contacting:

WestBow Press
A Division of Thomas Nelson
1663 Liberty Drive
Bloomington, IN 47403
www.westbowpress.com
1 (866) 928-1240

Unless otherwise noted, all Bible quotations are from Revised Standard
Version of the Bible, copyright 1952 [2nd edition, 1971] by the Division
of Christian Education of the National Council of Churches of Christ in
the United States of America. Used by permission. All rights reserved.

New Revised Standard Version Bible, copyright 1989, Division of Christian
Education of the National Council of the Churches of Christ in the
United States of America. Used by permission. All rights reserved.

Some Scripture quotations taken from the New English
Bible, copyright © Cambridge University Press and Oxford
University Press 1961, 1970. All rights reserved.

ISBN: 978-1-4908-1912-9 (sc)
ISBN: 978-1-4908-1913-6 (e)

Library of Congress Control Number: 2013922075

Printed in the United States of America.

WestBow Press rev. date: 1/7/2014

Acknowledgements

A draft of this book was sent to professor F. F. Bruce in early 1990. He replied encouragingly but unfortunately for me, he died the same year. I am, however, thankful for his input.

My wife of many years has supported me with her love, devotion, and cheerfulness. I could have done little without her.

I owe a huge debt of gratitude to my daughter Martha for the many hours she has spent making revisions and preparing this manuscript for publication.

I am also indebted to my son Timothy for valuable suggestions.

Contents

Chronology

Introduction

Most dates in antiquity are only probable; those below reflect my preference. The reader should find it helpful to have, at the beginning an outline, not only of Paul's history, but also the background of the whole New Testament.

Background History of New Testament Times

BC

ca 200	Septuagint, translation of Hebrew Scriptures into Greek, placed by Ptolemy II in his library in Alexandria; subsequently used by Jews in synagogues of Alexandria, Palestine and in the Greek-speaking diaspora generally
175 - 164	Seleucid king of Syria, Antiochus IV, in his effort to Hellenize his entire kingdom, decreed the suppression of Judaism, forbade the circumcision of male babies, destroyed synagogues and copies of the Torah, ordered slaughter of many Jews

41	assassination of Caligula, accession of Claudius; decree evicting Jews from Rome
	Herod Agrippa king of Judea
44	death of Herod Agrippa
51-52	Gallio proconsul of Achaia
62	execution of James at Jerusalem
66	beginning of war for Jewish independence
66-68	Jerusalem church flees to Pella
70	Titus captures Jerusalem, destroys temple

History of Paul
AD First Phase of Paul's Work

34-35	Stoning of Stephen - Paul heads for Damascus
35	Revelation-vision of Jesus near Damascus, conversion, Ananias baptizes Paul
35-38	Sojourn in Nabatea (Arabia), then back to Damascus, capture averted
38	visit to Peter at Jerusalem; trance in temple - "leave Jerusalem"
	commission to proclaim gospel to all nations (Acts 22.18)
	Paul goes (home) to Tarsus
	Barnabas brings Paul to Antioch; Paul spends a year at Antioch
39-40	gospel campaign with Barnabas to South Galatia, 4 churches
	Paul & Barnabas return to Antioch
	With Silas, Paul heads back to S Galatia, circumcises Timothy
	Paul goes on to Troas, meets Luke, Luke converted

Here Luke's order of events seems not to be historical;

Acts 15.1-29 should come at 18.22, as per reasons given in study below.

40-41   Macedonian call at Troas, with Luke etc to Philippi; Philippi, Thessalonica, Berea, churches planted in each;
         Paul writes to Thessalonian church from Berea (2 Thess).

Second Phase of Paul's Work

41-42   Athens - relatively few converts, no church planted
42   **1st revelation** - Corinth - "Christ died for our sins"
         Paul astounded, silent several days, perhaps a week
         2nd revelation - "End your silence. Fear nothing. I have many people in this city"
         In fear and trembling Paul proclaims "Christ died for our sins"
         Many Corinthians believe - gift of Holy Spirit - speaking in tongues (?)
         First truly Christian church planted in Corinth
         Paul writes again to Thessalonica (1 Thess)
         Another revelation - institution of Lord's supper (1 Cor 11.23)
42   Abundance of revelations - "caught up to third heaven"
43   Paul leaves Corinth, evangelizing in Galatia and elsewhere
51-52   Paul in Corinth again - Gallio proconsul

Third Phase of Paul's Work, Culminating in the Collection

52   Paul at Antioch, instruction as to "Christ died for our sins;"

Peter arrives; hears, accepts Paul's gospel of cross of Christ;

Happy table fellowship of everyone at Antioch;

Judaizers from Jerusalem arrive at Antioch;

Peter, fearing Jerusalem Judaizers, withdraws from table fellowship;

Barnabas follows Peter out, Paul rebukes Peter.

(unrecorded in scripture - Paul persuades Peter & Barnabas to return to table fellowship, ? pleading universality of cross-work of Christ ?)

52   Arrangement for private meeting near Jerusalem, James & John, Titus;

Near Jerusalem - private meeting, agreement: no circumcision of Titus;

James' request of Paul - "remember poor"; Paul agrees, plans collection;

Paul, Titus leave Jerusalem; starts writing to churches re collection;

Jerusalem council, Peter and James persuade elders; Decree written.

52   Paul gets news - "Galatian believers may accept circumcision;"

Paul writes letter to Galatians; continues gospel proclamation;

53-55   Paul writes 1 Corinthians;

56   writes 2 Corinthians, 14 years after "caught up to 3rd heaven;"

All NT documents were probably written before 70.

Study 1

Foreword

It is not generally realized that in the first two decades of Christianity two different gospels were preached. Many authors point out that the first believers from the day of Pentecost on, thought that Messiah Jesus would soon return to earth to set up a new kingdom of God on earth. The gospel we preach – Christ died for our sins – was not revealed to Paul until he arrived at Corinth about a dozen years after the crucifixion and resurrection of Jesus. (This book assumes the date of the crucifixion and resurrection to be 30 AD.) These studies inquire into what really happened in those dozen years.

Throughout the time of Jesus leading the twelve disciples around both Galilee and Judea, the twelve's notion (and that of most other Palestinian Jews) was that Messiah was to restore the Davidic kingdom and drive out the foreign oppressors from the holy land. Because Jesus' thoughts as to Messiah were totally different, the twelve were unable to understand his teachings. These were about a spiritual kingdom, not a material kingdom such as David's. The prophetic message as to the Messiah was totally misinterpreted and its spiritual character was almost completely missed.

The preaching of Messiah's imminent return was presented as Good News and thousands believed it. When Paul proclaimed the gospel of the cross of Christ as Good News thousands believed it too. Were all these believers equally saved? What were the implications for the day by day conduct of believers of each gospel?

"It is not the spiritual which is first but the physical" (1 Cor 15:46). This is also true of the two gospels. The first pertained to this earth only: its salvation was not that of an afterlife with Christ in heaven. The second offered a spiritual salvation, promising eternal life with Christ in glory. Was the forgiveness of sins offered in both gospels the same?

> "Conflict between Paul the apostle to the Greeks, and the narrow Jewish Christianity of the original disciples was the clue to the history of the apostolic age." (E. E. Ellis quoting F. C. Baur in "Paul" in *The New Bible Dictionary*, ed. J. D. Douglas, 947.)

What was the cause of that conflict? Could it have been averted?

Preparatory – From Abraham to John the Baptizer

The Jews' Scriptures provide summaries of their history up to the first century which is where our story will continue –

Now the LORD said to Abram, "Go from your country and your kindred and your father's house to the land that I will show you. And I will make of you a great nation, and I will bless you, and make your name great, so that you will be a blessing. I will bless those who bless you, and the one who curses you I will curse; and in you all the families of the earth shall be blessed." (Gen 12:1-3 NRSV)

I am the LORD who brought you from Ur of the Chaldeans, to give you this land to possess. (Gen 15:7)

A wandering Aramean was my father; and he went down into Egypt and sojourned there, few in number; and there he became a nation, great, mighty, and populous. And the Egyptians treated us harshly, and afflicted us, and laid upon us hard bondage. Then we cried to the LORD the God of our fathers, and the LORD heard our voice, and saw our affliction, our toil, and our oppression; and the LORD brought us out of Egypt with a mighty hand and an outstretched arm, with great terror, with signs and wonders; and he brought us into this place and gave us this land, a land flowing with milk and honey. And behold, now I bring the first of the fruit of the ground, which thou, O LORD, hast given me. (Deut 26:5-11).

But the people did not continue faithful to their God, as Ezra admits –

Nevertheless they were disobedient and rebelled against thee and cast thy law behind their back and killed thy prophets, who had warned them in order to turn them back to thee, and they committed great blasphemies. Therefore thou didst give them into the hand of their enemies, who made them suffer; and in the time of their suffering they cried to thee and thou didst hear them from heaven; and according to thy great mercies thou didst give them saviors who saved them from the hand of their enemies. But after they had rest they did evil again before thee, and thou didst abandon them to the hand of their enemies, so that they had dominion

3

over them; yet when they turned and cried to thee thou didst hear from heaven, and many times thou didst deliver them according to thy mercies. And thou didst warn them in order to turn them back to thy law. Yet they acted presumptuously and did not obey thy commandments, but sinned against thy ordinances, by the observance of which a man shall live, and turned a stubborn shoulder and stiffened their neck and would not obey. Many years thou didst bear with them, and didst warn them by thy Spirit through thy prophets; yet they would not give ear. (Neh 9:26-30)

> The prophets never cease to proclaim that this tragic situation which man's selfishness, pride and rebellion bring upon himself is always the occasion of God's grace in redemption. (Whale, *Christian Doctrine*, 63.)

The Jews' situation in the first century was similar to that in Ezra's day:

Behold, we are slaves this day; in the land that thou gavest to our fathers to enjoy its fruit and its good gifts, behold, we are slaves. And its rich yield goes to the kings whom thou hast set over us because of our sins; they have power also over our bodies and over our cattle at their pleasure, and we are in great distress. (Neh 9:36-37)

> The Old Testament writers … wrote history because they were convinced that they already knew the truth about God and his relation with men, and they wrote not as men concerned to establish a result by their writing, but as men who had already reached their conclusion and needed only to illustrate it, and bear witness to it. … what we must observe is that they wrote history as a confession

of faith. This is true of all the constituents of the Old Testament. … a confession of faith in God's saving acts on behalf of his people. (Barrett, *Luke the Historian*, 18.)

… the Old Testament betrays its own incompleteness and demands its own fulfillment. (Hoskyns & Davey, *The Fourth Gospel*, 391.)

A 20th century Jew wrote:

The true prototype of the Messiah was the second Israelite king, David, son of Jesse. His great political talents, by means of which he succeeded in unifying all the tribes of Israel and making them one great and powerful nation … were necessary to make him in the eyes of the people the greatest political savior of all those who defended Israel at any time. But his spiritual characteristics also fitted him to become in the eyes of the people the ideal type of the King-Messiah. … In fact, the Messianic expectation is the positive element in the message of the prophets. (Klausner, *The Messianic Idea in Israel*, 19-21.)

Beliefs and Expectations of First Century Jews

All Palestinian Jews to some extent believed in a Messianic solution. There were, it is true, many different doctrines of the Messiah but the variations were matters of detail and all rested on the unitary

Robert L. Greenhow

belief that foreign oppressors would be driven out and God alone would rule Israel. (Johnson, *History of Christianity*, 19.)

It is in this remarkable book (Daniel) that the hope for a bodily resurrection is plainly expressed, a hope that became a firm article of faith for the Pharisees and the people. The future of Israel is envisioned as a worldly kingdom in which all the saints who have fallen asleep will awake and participate. (Zeitlin, *Jesus and the Judaism of his Time*, 116.)

Messiah is thought of as an irresistible, wise and just ruler, who is 'mighty in his works and strong in the fear of God'; and the central violent contradiction between the primitive Christian kerygma and the Jewish Messianic hope is that which sets the crucified Messiah of Christian experience over against the triumphant hero of Jewish fantasy. (Manson, *The Servant-Messiah*, 36.)

As David was from Bethlehem, Bethlehem is the place from which the Messiah will arise. Accordingly, in sharp contrast to the present array of dislocations, or dependency, these the results of incursions of neighboring people, or of Roman conquerors, the hopes and wishes centered in the expectant advent of a divinely appointed individual through whom relief would come. … The future Davidic king could attain independence only through the defeat of the national foes. (Sandmel, *Judaism and Christian Beginnings,* Endnote, 451.)

Jesus

> And the Word became flesh. Flesh means man, not body ... He moves to history, to Jesus the Son of God. He moves also from the law delivered to Moses, from the Word of God inscribed on two tables of stone, to the Word of God written in the flesh of Jesus. What the law was powerless to effect, the incarnation of the Word of God has made known. (Hoskyns & Davey, *The Fourth Gospel*, 147.)

> John Wilkinson in the Notes of Principles of Biblical Interpretation, quotes E. C. Blackman, *Biblical Interpretation*, p 47: "What makes the Bible unique is its indispensability for the knowledge of that divine invasion of history; that is, its record of the life of Christ with the earlier events in Israel's history which provide the framework in which alone it can be seen in true perspective and without distortion." (Wilkinson, *Principles of Biblical Interpretation*, Notes.)

In the Nazareth synagogue the boy Jesus must have heard the first psalm, and quite possibly resolved to be one of those "blessed men." On hearing "Thy word have I hid in my heart" he would quite likely have silently decided to memorize much scripture. It should not be difficult to picture Jesus as being able to quote long passages of Isaiah, Jeremiah or many psalms, as well as the over-all story of the Old Testament. Before going to the Jordan to be baptized Jesus would not only have been familiar with all the scriptures, but also known how to apply them. He would also have known which Scriptures still remained to be fulfilled, to bring the story to its proper ending.

Furthermore Jesus and John (the Baptizer) in their 20s probably knew each other, and were aware of the angelic messages to their parents. By the time that John began to baptize, Jesus would have known that some of the Old Testament prophecies were yet to be fulfilled and may have wondered if he were to fulfill them as God's Messiah.

Sonship and Service in Israel

Sonship and service is illustrated first by God's telling Pharaoh (through Moses) *"Israel is my first-born son, … let my son go, that he may serve me."* (Ex 4:22-23) Again, Jesus spoke of a man with two sons, to both of whom he said to go to serve in his vineyard. (See Matt 21:28-30.) Also in the story of the prodigal son, the older son said, *"These many years I have served you … ."* (Luke 15:29) These illustrate that in Israelite families it was customary for the grown sons to serve in the family's interest. Paul refers to this custom: *"Timothy's worth you know, how as a son with a father he has served with me in the gospel."* (Phil 2:22)

Jesus had proved himself to be capable and competent by a flawless life, serving as a carpenter, trained by Joseph and then working alongside him "as a son with a father." Then later, when Joseph had apparently died, he worked to support himself and the family.

Jesus was One who had qualified himself as the Blessed man of the first Psalm, and One whose delight was in the

Law (that is, the Torah) of the Lord and in continual meditation of it, and who also could say *"Sacrifice and offering thou dost not desire; but thou hast given me an open ear. Burnt offering and sin offering thou hast not required. Then I said, "Lo, I come; … it is written of me; I delight to do thy will, O my God; thy law is within my heart"."* (Psalm 40:6-8)

> If the authority by which he acts and speaks be the authority of God, his divine Sonship adequately expresses the nature of his authority. (Hoskyns & Davey, *The Fourth Gospel*, 382.)

> Son of Man – Servant of God: this is one of the supreme paradoxes of Jesus' ministry. Judge and Vindicator – judged and vindicated; it is the same paradox in another form. In this way only could 'the many' be brought to their true place under the sovereign rule of God. (Dillistone *The Significance of the Cross*, 48.)

John Baptizing Jesus and Jesus' Temptations

When Jesus was baptized, he went up immediately from the water, and behold, the heavens were opened and he saw the Spirit of God descending like a dove, and alighting on him; and lo, a voice from heaven, saying, "This is my beloved Son, with whom I am well pleased." (Matt 3:16-17)

Empowered and sustained by what the divine Voice declared, knowing the Father's confidence, knowing too his having been delegated to act as his Father's agent, Jesus went into the wilderness to meet and ultimately reject and thus defeat the Adversary's numerous temptations.

When John had wanted Jesus to baptize him, Jesus had replied, *"Let it be so now* [that you baptize me]; *for thus it is fitting for us to fulfil all righteousness."* (Matt 3:15) (In the Old Testament when the reference is to God, the word 'righteousness' normally means 'faithfulness', that is, God is faithful in keeping his promises.) Jesus was telling John, "By being baptized I will identify myself with confessed sinners, and undertake to fulfill God's promises to his people."

> The task of John thus has two aspects. Negatively he had to destroy the confidence that the Messianic hope was a gilt-edged security from which every reasonably good Jew might expect to draw a dividend. Positively … he set out to create a New Israel to meet the coming Stronger One. He did not know … that it would need something thicker than Jordan water to bind the New Israel together, that the New Covenant that would create the New Israel must be sealed in Messianic blood. (Manson, *The Servant-Messiah*, 47.)

John had had messages from God: *"He who sent me to baptize with water said to me, 'He on whom you see the Spirit descend and remain, this is he who baptizes with the Holy Spirit.'"* (John 1:33)

From the heavenly Voice's message Jesus knew that henceforth his was to be a life of self-denying service. The wilderness temptations demonstrated this – "It is by his faith that the Just shall live." (See Hab 2:4) He would not use his so recently given power and authority to turn the stones into bread; by his faith in God he knew that at the right time God would give him what he needed. The God who declared that he was His Son and whom he was to serve would never cease to provide for him.

As Son, he was also God's heir, as affirmed later in Hebrews 1, and also as Jesus himself said, "All things have been entrusted to me" (See Matt 11:27; Luke 10:22 NEB uses "entrusted".) According to the promise of second Samuel 7, as scion of the house of David he was Messiah, Lord of all. But how was he to take possession of his inheritance? Was it by raising an army and by calling on God to send him legions of angels? But that would mean war and the killing of many; its effect would be the same as worshipping the devil.

As to the third wilderness temptation, this, found at http://epistle.us/articles/jesustemptation.html expresses its meaning very well –

> By jumping off the top of the Temple and floating down on the wings of angels, all the Jewish Temple worshipers would behold Jesus descending from Heaven, as they would have expected the Messiah to arrive. It would have been an amazing spectacle. People would have immediately worshiped Him as their King. His life from then on would have been of power, authority and glory. But isn't that why Jesus came to earth, to lead His people? The Jews were seeking such a Messiah that would come to save them. A strong mighty leader who would descend from Heaven and set up God's Kingdom on earth. But that is not why Jesus came. He didn't

Robert L. Greenhow

come for His own glory, but to be a humble servant
to do the purpose of God. And that purpose, was
to be a sacrifice for mankind. Again, He is taking a
step back from His own will to instead do the will
of God. (© 2009 Edrick)

Others have also written insightfully about the temptations:

Knowledge of possibilities leaves a man's judgment
about what is to be done unimpaired. Knowledge
of the real future would entail that the judgment
has already been taken, the crisis has already been
resolved. That which is essential to true freedom,
the personal resolution of a crisis, has thereby
been removed. Christ's life is not authentically
human if he is not called upon to decide for himself what is to be done, what it is that God wills
him to do in the various changing circumstances
of his life. In the brief scriptural phrase, "he was
tempted," we are made aware that Jesus was facing
a new encounter with God and a new encounter
with forces opposed to God. (De Rosa, *Christ and
Original Sin*, 64.)

In the temptations the Messiah is being invited
to take the center of the stage in one role or another. It is significant that each time the response
of Jesus puts God in the centre of the stage; and
each time the implication is made perfectly clear:
even the Messiah is only God's servant – indeed,
just because he is Messiah he must be pre-emi-
nently God's servant. The Messiah is the chief man
in Israel; then he must be the servant of all. But
above all he must be completely and unreservedly

the servant of the Lord. (Manson, *The Servant-Messiah*, 57.)

Our discussion ... has shown how widespread and how penetrating is the legacy of "original sin", a legacy which none of us can abjure. Christ the Deliverer came into the inheritance, and the implications of that must be honestly faced. If "he bore our sins" he must have known what sin meant. If he did not share the conditions of our humanity, then there was no real incarnation. "He did no sin neither was guile found in his mouth," and who, he asked, could convict him of sin? But the sinlessness which Christian faith attributes to him must not be interpreted colorlessly and negatively, as though it was effortless and automatic and not, from the human side, a moral achievement. His life was one of perfect obedience -- the obedience required at every developing stage of it and in all its changing situations -- and unbroken union with the will of God. (Barry, *The Atonement*, 70)

... the power which reconciles is ethical in quality. But to say this is to say -- when we speak of the man Christ Jesus -- that it is power which has been ethically earned and accumulated. The moral personality in which it is lodged and out of which it proceeds, has been formed and developed, like other moral personalities, through the duties and trials of our common human life. It could not have been formed and developed in any other way. (Denney, *Christian Doctrine of Reconciliation*, 23.)

To sum up, the wilderness temptations show that Jesus' life of service for God was to be a life of self-denial, of revealing the character of God (like Father, like Son) as compassionate, forgiving, healing, providing, always humbly serving or helping others, whatever their need or condition or circumstances.

Consequently, when the four friends of the paralytic lowered him from the dismantled roof into the presence of Jesus, *when Jesus saw their faith, he said to the paralytic, "My son, your sins are forgiven." Now some of the scribes were sitting there, questioning in their hearts, "Why does this man speak thus? It is blasphemy! Who can forgive sins but God alone?" And immediately Jesus, perceiving in his spirit that they thus questioned within themselves, said to them, "Why do you question thus in your hearts? Which is easier, to say to the paralytic, 'Your sins are forgiven,' or to say, 'Rise, take up your pallet and walk'? But that you may know that the Son of man has authority on earth to forgive sins"* --he said to the paralytic-- *"I say to you, rise, take up your pallet and go home." And he rose, and immediately took up the pallet and went out before them all.* (Mark 2:5-12)

The authority which the Son of man has on earth to forgive sins was included within the scope of the commission given in the heavenly "You are my Son." The heavenly Voice was the same One who had spoken in the Scriptures, and Jesus understood the Voice in the light of those Scriptures.

Messianic Expectations and Jesus' Fulfillment of Them

Jesus' authority was used very differently from what the Jews expected as to their Messiah. The following quotations illustrate this well.

> Glatzer writes "Jesus' preaching of the Kingdom of God did not refer to any of the Messianic expectations current at the time; the true understanding of Jesus' particular Messianic consciousness was beyond the grasp even of the immediate disciples". (Glatzer, in the Foreword to *The Pharisees*, by R. Travers Herford, 5.)

> The Messiah, it was expected, would condemn and destroy the unworthy. But now Jesus comes, seeking not the whole but the sick, not performers of the Law but publicans and harlots, the outcast, the despised, the sinking, the sunken. Representative as he was of the world's Judge, he yet turned with special tenderness to the guilty. It seemed unnatural, it seemed positively wrong and offensive, that he should bring God to the undeserving, like Zaccheus or the dying thief. To rejoice in a Christ like this was not easy, it is not easy now; for it means a new thought of God. (Macintosh, *Christian Experience of Forgiveness*, 98.)

> The Mission of Jesus … is directed first of all to those whom nobody wants, because they are no good to anybody. It is an offer of help to the foolish and the helpless, not an appeal for the support of

the wise and strong. So the first apostles are given as their message 'not a program for human action, but the proclamation of an act of God.' (Manson, *The Servant-Messiah*, 43.)

That is the way God is, Jesus insists. God is concerned with repentance, interested in lives that can be turned around -- about brothers and sisters who can be brought back into the family. (Juel, *Luke–Acts*, 38.)

People had to decide in Jesus' case, as in others, what that power meant. Was Jesus God's anointed, come to set the captives free? Or was he only a pretender, a false prophet, a friend of sinners and tax collectors intent on tearing down the tradition. The fateful question runs through the Gospel and Acts and provides drama to the very end. (Ibid., 47.)

In his final week in Jerusalem, Jesus began to tell the people this parable: *"A man planted a vineyard, and let it out to tenants, and went into another country for a long while. When the time came, he sent a servant to the tenants, that they should give him some of the fruit of the vineyard; but the tenants beat him, and sent him away empty-handed. And he sent another servant; him also they beat and treated shamefully, and sent him away empty-handed. And he sent yet a third; this one they wounded and cast out. Then the owner of the vineyard said, 'What shall I do? I will send my beloved son; it may be they will respect him.' But when the tenants saw him, they said to themselves, 'This is the heir; let us kill him, that the inheritance may be ours.' And they cast him out of the vineyard and killed him. What then will the owner of the vineyard do to them? He will come and destroy those tenants, and give the vineyard to*

*others." When they heard this, they said, "God forbid!" But he
looked at them and said, "What then is this that is written: 'The
very stone which the builders rejected has become the head of the
corner'?"* (Luke 20:9-17)

No explanation of the purpose of the death of Jesus
is given in the parable, but there are several implications of the greatest importance in forming an
opinion on this question: the position superior to
the prophets which is quietly assumed by Jesus,
the consciousness of a unique relationship of sonship, the conviction that he has been sent by God
as a final envoy to Israel, the recognition that rejection and death await him. There is also present the
consciousness that the rejection involves the judgment of Israel. (Taylor, *Jesus and his Sacrifice*, 107.)

The Jews now want to kill him for violating the
Sabbath and also for making himself equal to God.
The reply to this latter is a discourse (John 5:19-37)
which sets forth the relationship of the Son (Jesus)
to the Father (God). Jesus denies he is equal to
God. Rather it is through him that God has been
revealed, and an even greater revelation (his resurrection) will ensue. The Father, though, has entrusted judgment over men to the Son. (Sandmel,
Judaism and Christian Beginnings, 376.)

The short ministry, death and resurrection of Jesus are
summarized by Peter – *God anointed Jesus of Nazareth with
the Holy Spirit and with power; ... he went about doing good and
healing all that were oppressed by the devil, for God was with
him. And we are witnesses to all that he did both in the country
of the Jews and in Jerusalem.* (Acts 10:38-39)

When Jesus was nearing Jerusalem for the last time "… *they supposed that the kingdom of God was to appear immediately*." (Luke 19:11) This and remarks in the other gospels seem to have elicited this comment:

> (the people) … viewing Jesus' entry to Jerusalem as a 'triumphant' one, waved branches in his honor, as an expression of their expectation of the national liberty he would win for them. (Zeitlin, *Jesus and the Judaism of his Time*, 71.)

Note Jesus' words just before his midnight arrest: Jesus said to Peter, "*Put your sword back into its place; for all who take the sword will perish by the sword. Do you think that I cannot appeal to my Father, and he will at once send me more than twelve legions of angels? But how then should the scriptures be fulfilled, that it must be so?*" (Matt 26:52-54)

Jesus said to them, "Have you come out as against a robber, with swords and clubs to capture me? Day after day I was with you in the temple teaching, and you did not seize me. But let the scriptures be fulfilled." (Mark 14:48-49)

Jesus also said, "*I glorified thee on earth, having accomplished the work which thou gavest me to do.*" (John 17:4) Then the word he uttered from the cross was "*Tetelestai,*" (accomplished, fulfilled, completed, finished, done). He had "fulfilled all righteousness." Paul could write, *"all the promises of God find their Yes* [= their fulfillment] *in him."* (2 Cor 1:20)

> The rejection of Jesus by the Jews (before Pilate) has now reached its inevitable conclusion. They have declined the sovereignty of God, and abdicated their right to be his chosen people. By undertaking

the execution of the Messiah in defence of the majesty of Caesar the mystery of iniquity is consummated, and the blasphemy of the Jews is complete. (Hoskyns, & Davey, *The Fourth Gospel*, 525.)

On Calvary, *"Jesus uttered a loud cry, and breathed his last. And the curtain of the temple was torn in two, from top to bottom."* (Mark 15:37-38)

[re rending of temple veil] Did not God mean to show thereby, that from that time the temple was no longer his dwelling place? As the high priest rent his garment in view of any great offence, so God rends the veil which covers the place where he enters into communion with his people; that is to say, the Holy of Holies is no more; and if there is no Holy of Holies, then no Holy Place, and consequently no court, no altar, no valid sacrifices. The temple is profaned, and consequently abolished by God himself. The efficacy of sacrifice has henceforth passed to another blood, another altar, another priesthood. This is what Jesus had announced to the Jews in this form: "Put me to death, and by the very deed ye shall destroy the temple!". (Godet, *Luke*, 337.)

The death of Jesus is the completion of the scriptures. Having accomplished the will of God, the Christ longs for his return to the Father. (Hoskyns, & Davey, *The Fourth Gospel*, 531.)

Jesus was the one perfectly free man. He was fettered by no internal constraints of sin, and his will had not been weakened by sinning. Yet he and they were involved in a situation in which neither had complete freedom of action. The best things -- Roman justice, Jewish religion, and so on -- were corrupted and forced into the service of evil. "It is necessary that the Son of Man should suffer". The necessity lay within his own will -- the Cross could have been evaded; but it was a decision made by his own will within the total complex of circumstances by which his vocation was defined. (Barry, *The Atonement*, 73.)

... it is vicarious suffering that enters into the noblest spiritual achievement, and the Cross of Christ, considered simply as a fact of history, is its purest and highest instance. But why should we stop there, and rob God of the highest form of attainment which human life displays? Ought we not to expect that God will enter into this fellowship of suffering which all his creatures share – not as they do, by the sheer necessity of social relationship in its most realistic forms, but by that higher compulsion of love which is supremely his own? Such divine self-sacrifice is visible on the cross of Christ, if that cross is integrally and inclusively related to God. Then, and only then, is the true spiritual continuity of the universe fully manifest. (Robinson, *Redemption and Revelation*, 266.)

Man's own measure of responsibility for the abuse of his freedom remains. He is guilty of bringing upon God the sorrow of a defeated purpose, and the spiritual suffering entailed by the very existence of moral evil in a world which must constantly be sustained by God. (Ibid., 267.)

In the high and holy place, as in the cross below, sin makes its impact on holiness as suffering. Within the consciousness of God, sin cannot exist in any other form. The guilt of man actually consists in causing this suffering in the Holy One. (Ibid., 273.)

Peter, on the Day of Pentecost, proclaimed – *Jesus of Nazareth, a man attested to you by God with mighty works and wonders and signs which God did through him in your midst, as you yourselves know – this Jesus, delivered up according to the definite plan and foreknowledge of God, you crucified and killed by the hands of lawless men. But God raised him up, having loosed the pangs of death, because it was not possible for him to be held by it.* (Acts 2:22-24)

… it is clear from Mark's Gospel that to most of them (the many followers of Jesus) Jesus' conception of the Kingdom and of Messiahship remained a total mystery, and that he was more gravely embarrassed by their uncomprehending enthusiasm than by the enmity of the Pharisees. These supporters gave him their loyalty on the erroneous supposition that he was to be the traditional Son of David, and one of the great dangers of his ministry was that they should attempt to force him into the mould of their own messianic hopes. To them the Cross must have been as great a stumbling block as it was to any other Jew. (Caird, *Apostolic Age*, 88-89.)

Study 2

The Earliest Gospel

Clyde Manschreck writes:

> Although these writings differ in emphases, key beliefs or presuppositions that were basic to the life of the early community emerge:
>
> 1. At the center stands the Resurrection, a vindication of everything that Jesus taught and did …
> 2. The Resurrection convinced Jesus' followers that he was more than human, that he was divine, that in him God had acted. The Resurrection validated the authority of his teachings and miraculous deeds …
> 3. The Resurrection validated Jesus as Savior – his forgiveness of sins … (Manschreck, *History of Christianity in the World*, 14.)

… the resurrection and the appearances of the risen Christ finally convinced them [the disciples] that Messiah had indeed come and **would soon return in power and judgment to found his**

Kingdom. This was the message they went out into the streets of Jerusalem to proclaim. (Neil, *Galatians*, 4.)

That the imminent return of Messiah Jesus was the basis of the earliest gospel is maintained here.

On the road to Emmaus the risen Jesus met two disciples and after hearing their story, asked them, *"Was it not necessary that the Messiah should suffer these things and then enter into his glory?" Then beginning with Moses and all the prophets, he interpreted to them the things about himself in all the scriptures.* (Luke 24:26-27 NRSV)

For Messiah "to enter his glory" seemed to these two almost the same as their hope that Messiah was the one soon to redeem Israel.

The Emmaus disciples returned to Jerusalem and found the eleven gathered together and reported their experience with the risen Jesus. Soon Jesus himself appeared among them. If they had listened to his instructions, "to go to all nations and proclaim repentance and forgiveness of sins in my name" (Luke 24:47), they might not have been misled, after Jesus' ascension, into thinking he would very soon return to re-establish Israel as an independent kingdom.

* * * * *

Paul wrote: *"we ourselves boast of you in the churches of God for your steadfastness and faith in all your persecutions and in the afflictions which you are enduring. This is evidence of the righteous judgment of God, that you may be made worthy of the kingdom of God, for which you are suffering – since indeed God deems it just to repay with affliction those who afflict you, and to grant rest with us to you who are afflicted, when the Lord Jesus is revealed from heaven with his mighty angels in flaming fire, inflicting vengeance upon those who do not know God and upon those who do not obey the gospel of our Lord Jesus. They shall suffer the punishment of eternal destruction and exclusion from the presence of the Lord and from the glory of his might, when he comes on that day … "* (2 Thess 1:4-10)

Two points deserve notice. First, God is still thought of in the Old Testament character, violent and vengeful, repaying evil with evil, affliction with affliction. This is in total contrast with his other letter to them as we shall see. Second, Paul says that the believers can "be made worthy of the kingdom of God." That might be possible of a kingdom here on earth, which he was then thinking of, but it contrasts with what he a little later learned.

Within a few months of writing the letter just quoted, Paul wrote the same people, the believers at Thessalonica another letter. In the interval he learned, by revelation, the cross gospel. In it he told them, "See that none of you repays evil for evil, but always seek to do good to one another and to all."

What Jesus told Peter just before being taken in Gethsemane, about God sending him more than twelve legions of angels, contrasted with "but how then would the scriptures be fulfilled?" To Jesus his cross and resurrection would fulfill the scriptures; to Peter the restoration of David's kingdom would fulfill the scriptures. Peter's was a literal reading, completely misunderstanding the scriptures. Jesus' was a spiritual reading, revealing God's purpose, as does Paul's gospel of the cross.

The first gospel is one of self-seeking, self-serving. The true gospel of the cross is self-giving, self-sacrificing. The first is that of "saving one's life;" the second of "losing one's life."

As to daily conduct, Paul wrote: *let your manner of life be worthy of the gospel of Christ, so that whether I come and see you or am absent, I may hear of you that you stand firm in one spirit, with one mind striving side by side for the faith of the gospel, and not frightened in anything by your opponents. This is a clear omen to them of their destruction, but of your salvation, and that from God. For it has been granted to you that for the sake of Christ you should not only believe in him but also suffer for his sake, engaged in the same conflict which you saw and now hear to be mine. So if there is any encouragement in Christ, any incentive of love, any participation in the Spirit, any affection and sympathy, complete my joy by being of the same mind, having the same love, being in full accord and of one mind. Do nothing from selfishness or conceit, but in humility count others better than yourselves. Let each of you look not only to his own interests, but also to the interests of others.* (Phil 1:27-2:4)

The Christian has a high standard for day to day conduct; the 'Jesus messianist,' on the other hand, while awaiting the return of Messiah, lives day by day as he has been accustomed to live since his youth.

Other writers share their thoughts on the imminent return gospel:

> What was the basic content of the expectations? Foremost, that the Messiah would restore Judean independence through destroying the power of Rome. He would crush all enemies so that Israel would emerge as God's unique, elect nation. He

would assume the throne of Israel as the son of David. ... He would gather in the dispersed of Israel, miraculously bringing them back to the Holy Land (as in Isaiah 43:5-7). He would usher in the Great Judgment, thereby inaugurating a new age, the World to Come. (Sandmel, *Judaism and Christian Beginnings*, 208.)

The disciples believed that they had personally witnessed the beginning of the actual Resurrection. It was this belief that in the minds of the disciples transformed the crucified Jesus into the Messiah, who would soon triumphantly return. The belief in Jesus' resurrection became, in the words of Jacob Jocz, 'the cornerstone upon which the faith in the Messiahship of Jesus was built'. Paul's whole theology centers round this fact. It is not the cross but the Resurrection which is the starting point of Pauline thought. It was also the Resurrection which became the kerygma of the primitive church. That Christ was risen from the dead was their *'evangelion'*. (Zeitlin, *Jesus and the Judaism of his Time*, 164.)

The only article of faith distinguishing the Nazarenes from other devout Jews was their belief in the suffering Messiah who would soon reappear on the Day of Judgment at the right hand of Power to establish the Kingdom of Heaven, which naturally included the restoration of the independent kingdom of Israel. (Ibid., 169.) (This is well stated, except that 'suffering' could be replaced by 'risen'. The earliest messianic community thought of Jesus as risen, and 'suffering' only as prelude to resurrection. RLG)

Robert L. Greenhow

... the early church from its very beginning explicitly regarded (Jesus) as the fulfilment of the Jewish Messianic expectation ... . (Filson, *The New Testament Against its Environment*, 17.)

The message and claim of both Jesus and the apostolic church was that in what he said and did, God himself was definitely active to bring his providential purpose to fulfilment. God sent him; God was acting in and through him; God was doing something which called for a response of faith and acceptance. God did this within Judaism. He did so uniquely and authoritatively in Jesus. (Ibid., 19.)

... the Jesus community which first took shape after Easter understood these events as the beginning of the end of the world and the dawn of the rule of God. (Hengel, *The Atonement*, 66.)

The earliest Christians regarded the outpouring of the Spirit as a sign that the end of the world was at hand. (Haenchen, *Acts of the Apostles*, 143.)

The early church was thinking in terms of a speedy return of Christ to wind up the present order and to bring in a completely new order. (Manson, *Ethics and the Gospel*, 74.)

The Pauline Christians believe in one God, sole creator of the universe and ultimate judge of all human actions. In most respects their monotheism is exactly that of Judaism: they worship not the highest God but the only God and regard the deities of other cults as nonexistent or as antigods, demons. Yet they also accord to the crucified and resurrected Messiah, Jesus, some titles and functions that in the Bible and Jewish tradition were attributed only to God.

The Pauline world view is eschatological. The Christians believe that the coming of Jesus, his crucifixion and resurrection, have already set in motion a shift in the order of the world. They expect very soon an end of the present age, the return of Jesus, and the final judgment of both humans and cosmic powers. (Meeks, *The First Urban Christians*, 190.)

After his death his adherents, at first despairing, united under the lasting influence of his personality, and after they had seen him in visions as risen from the dead, they expected that he would return as the Messiah, the "Son of Man," on the clouds of heaven, and would set up the Kingdom. (Bultmann, *Jesus and the Word*, 91.)

In the early chapters of The Acts, we cannot escape from the dominant feeling of exultation which filled the hearts of the disciples. ... For the moment, it seems, they were not so concerned with what the death of Christ had effected but rather with the new life which had been made available through his resurrection. (Dillistone, *The Significance of the Cross*, 29.)

Paul's discussion is dominated by the idea of the imminent return of Christ and the establishment of a Messianic reign on earth, which for most of those he is addressing will occur this side of the grave. (Robinson, *In the End God*, 104.)

That beyond which nothing can happen had already happened. This goes to explain the prevailing certainty among the New Testament writers that time must shortly come to an end. (Ibid., 70.)

The historical events of that weekend have about them a quality of uniqueness for which there is neither comparison nor precedent -- not discontinuous with what went before, yet an utterly new start and new beginning. They inaugurate, as the believers said, a new age, a new heaven and a new earth. It has been said lately that the Resurrection is "as ultimate and unique an event as that of creation itself. We cannot see the relation either of history or of nature to the Father except across the mystery of the Resurrection of Christ." (Barry, *The Atonement*, 183.)

In the book of Acts this witness to the resurrection is the key witness. ... We are so indoctrinated with the central importance of the death of Jesus that it is hard for us to realize that this was not the accent in the apostolic age. The resurrection was central; even the death of Jesus was seen and interpreted in the light of the resurrection. The basic witness of the apostles was to the resurrection of Jesus. They had seen the risen Christ; they could testify with complete confidence that he had risen from the dead. (Filson, *Three Crucial Decades*, 37.)

The divine act described in the apostolic preaching was an act of forgiveness, and the preaching closed with a summons to accept what God had freely offered. In the theology of Paul and later New Testament writers this forgiveness was especially connected with the cross. Is there then any evidence to show that this connexion had been made in the earliest days of the Christian movement? Many scholars have asserted that in the speeches ascribed to Peter in Acts there is no such evidence, and have concluded that the Cross did not have the central place in the gospel according to Jerusalem which it certainly had in the gospel according to Paul. (Caird, *The Apostolic Age*, 39.)

There is in Acts less emphasis on the saving benefit of Jesus' death than some Christians suppose. (Filson, *Three Crucial Decades*, 25.)

It is astonishing that none of these commentators continued, and wrote that the believers preached what they believed, except William Neil.

Stephen

Stephen's story is given in Acts 6:8-8:1.

Note the charge against Stephen: *This man never ceases to speak words against this holy place and the law; for we have heard him say that this Jesus of Nazareth will destroy this place, and will change the customs which Moses delivered to us.* (Acts 6:13-14)

31

"This holy place" and "this place" refer to the temple and to Jerusalem; Luke describes the charges as false. Jesus predicted the temple's destruction but did not say that he would destroy it.

> [Stephen's] speech is essentially a vehement diatribe against the Jewish people [i.e. official Judaism] which is eternally rebellious against the divine will. Stephen especially condemns the temple, which Solomon built in defiance of God's will: 'However, the Most High does not live in houses made by men' (Acts 7:48, NEB). The meaning of such a statement becomes clear if it is remembered that in the usage of Hellenistic Judaism the word *'cheiropoietos'* (made by man's hand) is more or less the technical designation for idols. In the LXX this term is often used to translate the Hebrew word *'elil'* which means idol. To reject the temple because it was made by human hands is thus to rank it together with idolatry. This is condemnation of sacrificial worship, of which the temple was the exclusive locus. It is significant that the only allusion which Stephen made to sacrifices was in regard to the golden calf, which he characterized also as 'the thing their hands had made.' Stephen apparently saw no difference between the sacrifices offered to false gods and those offered in that temple, ostensibly to honor the Almighty. (Simon, *Jewish Sects at the Time of Jesus*, 99.)

The earliest Christian 'Hebrews' in Jerusalem, not to mention those in Jewish Palestine, remained relatively unaffected by these 'internal' controversies within the Greek-speaking synagogues of Jerusalem (i.e. those re Stephen and the persecutions and the exodus of Hellenist Christians). (Hengel, *The Pre-Christian Paul*, 77.)

The real source of Stephen's doctrine was the teaching of Jesus. Up to this point the Jerusalem Christians had emphasized those elements in the teaching of Jesus which united them with Judaism. Stephen drew attention to those elements which had brought Jesus into controversy with the religious authorities, and it was no accident that the charge brought against the first Christian martyr was the charge already brought against his Lord. (Caird, *The Apostolic Age*, 86.)

In Stephen's speech there is a constant rebuke of Israel's constant missing the significance of the working of God because of its emphasis upon externals. (Longenecker, *Paul, Apostle of Liberty*, 275.)

To get a true idea of the significance of Stephen's message, we must note several things. First, as noted previously, the twelve wanted nothing to do with it. They were absent, conspicuously so. They must have known Stephen's ideas and shared none of them. Some features of his speech (see Acts 7:2-53):

1. There is no mention of Jesus as Messiah.
2. David, Messiah's prototype, is mentioned only to say that he was not to build "a habitation for the God of Jacob." (verse 46)
3. Though the charge against Stephen concerned Jerusalem and the temple, in reviewing Israel's history he speaks of many places outside Palestine.

But he ignores the Holy Land, Jerusalem and even the temple, except, at the end, to suggest that it ought not to have been built, or at least not rebuilt (quoting Isaiah 66).

4. The law is mentioned only to say his hearers hadn't kept it.
5. There is no mention of the covenant except by the unusual term "living oracles." (verse 38)
6. Sacrifice is only to Aaron's golden calf (verses 41-42) ("Did you offer to me slain beasts and sacrifices" quoting Amos 5:25-27).
7. The tabernacle is of Moloch. (verse 43)
8. There is nothing of Jesus' imminent return.
9. "I will remove you beyond Babylon." (verse 43)

No wonder that his audience was incensed and furious; no wonder that the twelve disciples, wanting to be known as observant Jews, dissociated themselves from Stephen, a virtual heretic from their point of view. To Stephen, Jesus was "the Son of Man," of Daniel's chapter 7 vision, the Son of man who is given universal rule. Stephen saw that Jesus was for the world, the whole of humanity, not to be confined to one nation. In this respect Stephen foreshadowed Paul and John, as well as Luke himself. Note how Luke connects Paul with Stephen's stoning. Was he thinking of what he had read in Paul's letters, as in first Corinthians 15:9, Galatians 1:13 & 23, and First Timothy 1:13? (As Paul's companion for many months Luke would probably have had access to Paul's copies of his letters.)

At this point Luke writes that a great persecution of the church began with Saul (Paul's previous name) invading many houses and committing many believers to prison. Not content with that, he obtained authorization from the

high priest to arrest any disciples whom he might find in
the synagogues in Damascus. But as he neared that city,
Saul was suddenly stopped by a blinding flash of light
from above, and a Voice saying, "I am Jesus," and accusing him of persecuting him. In Damascus, Ananaias was
divinely instructed to tell Saul that he was chosen by God
to take the gospel of Jesus to the nations. Then Saul went
into Nabatea (Arabia). (See full story in Acts 9:1-25)

It was as clear to Paul then (before his conversion)
as it was to Stephen – unlike the Twelve and the
Jerusalem Christians generally – that Christianity
and Judaism would not mix. As a zealous Pharisee,
Paul was bound to try to stamp out a movement
which challenged Israel's claim to be the People of
God. ... At all events the issue for Paul was plain.
Jesus had been condemned and put to death for
blasphemy, in accordance with the Law. In the light
of the most sacred God-given truth which had been
revealed to Israel uniquely among the nations, and
to which Paul was heart and soul committed, Jesus
was under the curse of God (Galatians 3:13). But if,
as the Christians said, God had raised Jesus from
the dead – and admittedly no one had been able to
produce his dead body to refute this unthinkable
claim – then God would have been revoking his
own most holy Law and making it no longer absolute and infallible. Moreover, Jesus could not have
been the Messiah, for the Pharisees maintained
that when Israel as a nation lived in perfect obedience to the Law, Messiah would come, and not
before. But the people were far from obeying the
Law and even a devout Pharisee like Paul himself
had found it impossible. This was why the claims

of the Christians were to the zealous Paul mon-
strous and preposterous. And this was why his
sudden vision on the Damascus road of Jesus not
as the crucified felon but as the Christ victorious
over death struck him senseless and temporarily
blinded him. (Neil, *Galatians*, 26-28.)

For the next three years Saul must have pondered the consequences and implications of Jesus having been raised
from the dead. Was he then Messiah after all? Then he
returned to Jerusalem. During the two weeks he spent
in Jerusalem, in the temple in a trance he heard Jesus say,
*"Make haste and get quickly out of Jerusalem, because they will
not accept your testimony about me. ... I will send you far away
to the Gentiles."* (Acts 22:17-21)

The Cornelius Episode – (Acts 10–11:18)

While visiting Simon in Joppa Peter was given a mysteri-
ous vision of a great sheet, let down by four corners upon
the earth. In it were all kinds of animals and reptiles and
birds of the air. And a voice came to him, *"Rise, Peter; kill
and eat."* But Peter said, *"No, Lord; for I have never eaten anything that is common or unclean."* And the voice came to him
again a second time, *"What God has cleansed, you must not call
common."* (Acts 10:13-15)

Peter was perplexed about its meaning when messengers
from a centurion, Cornelius, in Caesarea arrived. Peter
listened to their story and invited them in to spend the
night. The next day Peter and some Jews of Joppa went;
on arrival at Cornelius' house, he found many gathered to

hear what Peter had to say. He began, *"I truly understand that God shows no partiality, but in every nation anyone who fears him and does what is right is acceptable to him."* and continued, telling of Jesus' going around healing the sick and curing those who were oppressed by the devil … *They put him to death by hanging him on a tree; but God raised him on the third day and allowed him to appear, not to all the people but to us who were chosen by God as witnesses, and who ate and drank with him after he rose from the dead. He commanded us to preach to the people …* " (Acts 10:34-42 NRSV)

They listened and while Peter was still speaking the Holy Spirit came on them and they all began speaking in tongues, which gave Peter much surprise! God had given Cornelius and his guests the same gift that he himself had received!

Back in Jerusalem the circumcision party questioned Peter, "Why did you go into the house of uncircumcised men and eat with them?"

Peter replied telling his story from the beginning … that he and six brothers went into Cornelius' house and told the story of Jesus (as above). And while Peter was still speaking the Holy Spirit came on them and they all began speaking in tongues. Then he *"remembered the word of the Lord, how he said, 'John baptized with water, but you shall be baptized with the Holy Spirit.' If then God gave the same gift to them as he gave to us* [the 120 in the upper room] *when we believed…* [in Jesus as Lord and Messiah, Peter reasoned], *who was I that I could withstand God?"* (Acts 11:16-17)

When they heard this they were silenced. And they glorified God, saying, "Then to the Gentiles also God has granted repentance unto life." (Acts 11:18)

> This passage (about Cornelius) is a meditation on universalism, the philosophy of the destiny of Christianity within the history of all humanity. The Christian concept of universalism – salvation for those within, equal opportunity to join for those without – is a direct result of the historical issue of the Gentiles entering the Christian community and the attendant problems for Jewish purity laws. It is a logical and proper association, reflecting the social reality of the Gentile presence, though it is almost never discussed in that context by church historians. (Segal, *Rebecca's Children*, 165.)

* * * * *

Legalism dies hard. Law is popular: "Do this and you will live." In contrast, grace is unpopular and poorly understood; it is too simple: "Accept God's offer of eternal life; it's free, no strings attached." The first century antipathy of LAW towards grace remains strong two millennia later. "The law was given by Moses; grace and truth came by Jesus Christ."

In Luke's account, soon after Stephen's death, some of his friends scattered and preached the gospel elsewhere. Philip preached in Samaria with positive results; then he was directed to the Ethiopian eunuch who also accepted the gospel message; next he headed back north to Caesarea, but didn't arrive before Peter, by divine arrangement. Philip could have been used by the Spirit for the conversion of

Cornelius and his guests quite as well as Peter. why then was Philip kept from arriving before Peter? The answer is two-fold; Peter needed a reminder not needed by Philip, and Peter was a most acceptable personage in Jerusalem whereas there Philip was *persona non grata*.

Peter was himself convinced by the results of his own preaching, and surprised too, on witnessing the effects of the gift of the Holy Spirit to Cornelius and his guests, seeing and hearing them speaking in tongues. This was a "demonstration of the Spirit" in those converts speaking in tongues, proof to him that this was a powerful divine work. This was a needed feature for Peter's education.

What better answer could one want to any question as to whether or not Gentiles, as uncircumcised, could be admitted to God's community of those who believed that Jesus was Messiah? Peter's conviction is seen in his answer to those who wanted the benefits of Messiah's reign restricted to Jews only. On learning that the Gentiles had obviously been given the Holy Spirit they were silenced but their stalwart Jewishness kept them from being genuinely convinced. Of course, they didn't want to be convinced.

This repeated "speaking in tongues" was to be evidence to those already 'in' that those who were imagined to be 'inadmissibles' were acceptable to God and welcome 'inside', just as much as those, like the circumcision party at Jerusalem, who prided themselves that they were God's chosen people to the exclusion of others. These were legalists who would not accept 'intruders'. They made observance of the law of Moses the criterion, rather than the currently active Holy Spirit. They were the ones who refused to acknowledge that the Spirit of grace was working in human hearts, irrespective of national origin, Jew or Gentile, and they kept the earliest communities in a state of turmoil and disunity.

When Peter said, "Who was I that I should withstand God?" the circumcision party was silenced. And they glorified God, saying, "To Gentiles also God has granted repentance unto life." Probably it was not the silenced circumcision party who thus glorified God, but rather those not of that party. But Luke wants not to emphasize disunity in the messianic community so his language is ambiguous. Much later it becomes clear that the circumcision party included almost the whole community.

Expansion of the Gospel beyond Palestine

Several authors have suggested that the Jerusalem *ekklésia* regarded the Cornelius incident as an isolated event, hopefully not to be repeated. In fact, as Luke makes clear, it was God's last call to Peter and the twelve to begin following Jesus' instructions to take the gospel to the world. Seeing no one from Jerusalem made a move to go to the Gentiles, as Luke's narrative indicates, others, unnamed, took the gospel abroad. It was men of Cyprus and Cyrene (Acts 11:20), far from Jerusalem and Judea, who preached to Greeks at Antioch, many of whom believed.

So began a messianic community at Antioch of both Jews and Gentiles as such, with the tacit condoning by the Jerusalem community of equality of Jew and Gentile (or practical abolishing of any distinction between them). Paul spent a year in such a fellowship of converted Jews and Gentiles virtually ignoring the ritual law. This indiscriminate fellowship was simply practiced apparently with no further development of an explicit doctrine of the abolishing of Jew-Gentile distinction than that of Acts 11:18 - *"Then to the Gentiles also God has granted repentance unto life."*

Some may wonder why the circumcision party didn't send a few men to Antioch to persuade the congregation there to see to it that all the Gentile believers were circumcised. Probably they realized both that the rebuff they had suffered in the Cornelius matter was too recent, and that Barnabas was probably the man the Antiocheans looked to more than anyone else. They knew that in Antioch he was too strong for them. Barnabas had seen that the new believers were all getting along together, taking no notice of their differing racial origins, even happily eating together.

> The evangelists were persecuted men, unauthorized by any save the Holy Spirit that was in them, and they brought the gospel as far as Antioch. Inspired by their success, the apostles began to follow their example, but only on two occasions did they think fit to intervene in the work of the missionary pioneers. On both occasions a change of policy was involved, once when Philip preached for the first time to the half-pagan Samaritans, once when men of Cyprus and Cyrene began to preach to Gentiles (Acts 8:14; 11:22ff). (Caird, *The Apostolic Age*, 71.) (But the apostles did not follow their example; it was Hellenist believers who did so. RLG)

> The teaching of the disciples in Jerusalem contained no elements foreign to Judaism. It was probably considered by the Jewish authorities as the erroneous application to Jesus of opinions which, rightly or wrongly, were widely held among the Jews; but nothing in it represented concession to Hellenism. As soon as Hellenism was suspected the Christians were at once driven out. In Antioch, on the other hand, much that was distinctly Jewish was abandoned, and Hellenistic thought adopted, so that Jesus became the divine center of a cult. It is incredible that he should have been so regarded by the Jews of Jerusalem; it is impossible that he should not have been by Gentiles. (Lake, *Landmarks in the History of Early Christianity*, 56.)

> The universalist christology of the Hellenists, who now saw the risen and exalted Jesus as the Lord of all men, rather than the exclusive Messiah of Israel, exercised pressure towards a universal mission without the limitations of the law. (Hengel, *Acts & the History of Earliest Christianity*, 104.)

Paul

Paul's coming into the picture begins the truly aggressive proclamation of the gospel to the Gentiles. For three years he stayed away from Jerusalem but proclaimed in the synagogues in Damascus that Jesus is the Messiah, Son of God. There were other believers in Messiah Jesus but none of them, not even Ananias, seemed interested in preaching the gospel. Paul was, and so vigorously that some Jews plotted to kill him. However, he escaped, went to Jerusalem and spent two weeks with Peter. (see Acts 9:23-26)

No doubt Paul wanted to learn from Peter all he could of Jesus, especially of Jesus' death and of the resurrection appearances, of what Jesus had said after his resurrection. Probably Paul told Peter of his own conversion on the road to Damascus, and of his gaining many converts in the synagogue there, as well as the story of his escape from Damascus.

Thinking that someone else might be able to tell him more, Paul may have asked others who had seen Jesus after his resurrection, and learned that more than 500 believers had seen him, probably in Galilee. But as to what Paul learned of Jesus' words, we know nothing.

Paul arrived at Antioch via Tarsus, where Barnabas found him and brought him to Antioch. (see Acts 11:26) Barnabas saw that Paul would be a valuable asset in teaching and preaching the gospel. Paul may have told Barnabas of his being divinely commissioned in the temple, to take the Gospel to the nations. After a year there teaching the disciples along with others, the Lord gave instructions through the Holy Spirit that Barnabas and Paul were to be devoted to the Lord's work.

Development of the Content of the Earliest Proclamations

Paul preached in the synagogue at Pisidian Antioch, as we read in Acts 13, that the Gentiles were invited to acknowledge Jesus as their Messiah as well as the Jews, without being required to be circumcised or observe Jewish law or ritual:

... Let it be known to you therefore, brethren, that through this man [Jesus] *forgiveness of sins is proclaimed to you, and by him every one that believes is freed from everything from which you could not be freed by the law of Moses.* (Acts 13:38-39)

This is first of all addressed to Paul's "brethren," the Jews, so that they too could be freed from all necessity of continuing to observe the oral law or ritual. And the "every one" excludes none, of whatever race or nation.

What is practiced sometimes comes before any stated reason for it. The practice at Antioch was for converted Jews and converted Gentiles to fellowship together. Paul apparently developed a doctrine from this practice; this is what he preached – "through this man – the risen Jesus – by him everyone who believes is freed from everything from which you could not be freed by the law of Moses." This not only offers divine forgiveness equally to Jew and Gentile without reference to Moses' law, but announces the impotence of that law to liberate anyone from sin and its consequences. The public announcement of the equality of Jew and Gentile, and the inability of the Mosaic law to save are huge advances. Thus began a long series of developments in Pauline doctrine. And this is what Paul preached in his gospel of the imminent return of Messiah.

In Acts there is no explicit statement of any gospel; reasons for Luke's omission of any statement are given below. But there can be no doubt that the twelve, and others too, preached what William Neil says, "Messiah has come

(Jesus' resurrection from the dead confirms his messianic role) and will soon return in power to establish his kingdom." This is what was preached and believed in Antioch, and everywhere Paul went: the gospel of Messiah's imminent return to establish a Davidic type of kingdom, or, perhaps better, the Kingdom of God (which, in the minds of the believers, were identical).

Various more modern authors write about the early church practices and beliefs as follows.

> One cannot read far in the letters of Paul and his disciples without discovering that it was concern about the internal life of the Christian groups in each city that prompted most of the correspondence. The letters also reveal that those groups enjoyed an unusual degree of intimacy, high levels of interaction among members, and a very strong sense of internal cohesion and of distinction both from outsiders and from "the world". (Meeks, *The First Urban Christians*, 74.)

> These examples indicate that the Pauline groups were having to discover workable means for drawing boundaries around themselves. The Pauline school had self-consciously abandoned the rules of purity that helped to maintain the social boundaries of the Jewish communities, for in a community composed largely of former gentiles these rules were dysfunctional – and, for Paul, they appeared to deny the newness of the gospel of the crucified and risen Messiah. (Ibid., 103.)

(quoting E. A. Judge) "Security and hospitality when travelling had traditionally been the privilege of the powerful, who had relied upon a network of patronage and friendship, created by wealth." The letters of recommendation disclose the fact that these domestic advantages were now extended to the whole household of faith, who are accepted on trust, though complete strangers. (Ibid., 109.)

Perhaps the relatively greater number of women converts is explainable by the lack of need for circumcision. The demands of Paul for conversion did not include circumcision, and conceivably the success of the Christian missionary enterprise profited enormously from the absence of this requirement. (Sandmel, *Judaism and Christian Beginnings*, 231.)

... in (Luke's) view there was never any conflict between Christians and Judaism; when antagonism arose, it was that Jews were over and against Christians and Christianity, these unremittingly loyal to Judaism. Indeed for Luke, Christianity is the true Judaism, the unbroken legatee of the Judaism of the past. Luke is concerned that not only Christians should understand this, but also that the Romans, especially Roman officials, should understand this too. (Ibid., 363.)

His followers believed that he had been resurrected. They came to view his messiahship not in the normal Jewish way of a single climactic event, but rather as divisible into two aspects – first, his initial coming, which was preparatory and had already taken place, for he had ascended into heaven; and next, he was soon to return in his 'second coming'. This second coming would be the climax of history, and usher in the events of the Great Judgment. The idea of the second coming is of crucial significance in New Testament writings. (Ibid., 307.)

The Synagogue mitzvah system (which Paul speaks of as 'works of the Law') is precisely that reliance by man on himself which Paul considers utterly and totally wrong and ineffective. It follows then, that Jews are unable to earn God's favor; therefore they are not better off, despite their inheritance of Scripture, than are the Gentiles who have no such inheritance. It is to Gentiles … that Paul feels himself appointed. He offers them not obedience to the Laws of Moses, but the opportunity of receiving the Holy Spirit. (Ibid., 313.)

The writer shows from the position of the believing Jew how the revelation of the Son of God deals with these facts finally. 'Jesus the Son of God' (4:14, cf Acts 9:20) fulfilled the destiny of man, Himself true man, by bringing humanity to the throne of heaven. He fulfilled this destiny through suffering and death, bearing Himself the last consequences of sin and overcoming death through death. (Westcott, *Epistle to Hebrews*, lvi.)

Through such a view of Christ's work, illuminated in the fuller view of His Person, the Hebrew believer, in short, found his disappointments unexpectedly transformed. He recognized the majesty of Christ's spiritual triumph. He perceived the divine significance of Christ's sufferings, and through that he perceived also the interpretation of the sufferings of men … .(Ibid., lvii) (Here Westcott ignores the fact that the Jewish believers in Jerusalem had no such exalted thoughts, being still "zealous for the Law". RLG)

There is unquestionably a sense in which Origen is right in saying the thoughts of the Epistle (Hebrews) are the thoughts of Paul. The writer shows the same broad conception of the universality of the Gospel as the Apostle of the Gentiles, the same grasp of the age-long purpose of God wrought out through Israel, the same trust in the atoning work of Christ, and in his present sovereignty. He speaks with the same conscious mastery of the Divine Counsel, But he approaches each topic from a different side. … He speaks as one who step by step had read the fulfilment of the Old Covenant in the New without any rude crisis of awakening or any sharp struggle with traditional errors. His Judaism had been all along the Judaism of the prophets and not of the Pharisees, of the Old Testament and not of the schools. (Ibid., lxxviii.)

After his first tour with Barnabas when four churches were established, Paul spent "no little time" in Antioch. After the disagreement with Barnabas about Mark, Paul and Silas, "commended by the brotherhood to the grace of the Lord," went "through Syria and Cilicia," visiting Derbe and Lystra. There Paul found Timothy, "well spoken of by the brotherhood at Lystra and Iconium," circumcised him and had him join Silas as another companion in the proclamation of the gospel. Then at Troas Luke was converted. (Acts 14-17)

(Luke and Paul seem to have been strongly attracted to each other; Luke learned much from Paul and Paul became Luke's hero. Probably it was through Paul's influence that Luke wrote his gospel and then Acts.)

In a vision Paul saw a Macedonian saying *"Come over to Macedonia and help us."* (Acts 16:9) Paul and his companions judged this to be the call of God to take the gospel there, so they all crossed over and came to Philippi, which apparently was where Luke made his home.

At Philippi, then at Thessalonica and Berea churches were founded, all within not many months. Then, because of the threat of serious harassment by Jews, Paul went south to Athens. Here in the market Paul's comments in conversation so aroused the curiosity of the Athenians that they invited him to present his thoughts in a lecture, which he did on the Areopagus. He ended his lecture with this statement: *"God ... commands all men everywhere to repent, because he has fixed a day on which he will judge the world in righteousness by a man whom he has appointed, and of this he has given assurance to all men by raising him from the dead."* (Acts 17:30-31)

In Luke's summary of Paul's message, Jesus' resurrection is the important point. Note that no interpretation is given of Jesus' death. These two features (equality of Jew and Gentile, and the inability of the Mosaic law to save) are to be seen also in Paul's discourse in Pisidian Antioch (Acts 13). This is characteristic of the 'imminent return of

Messiah Jesus' gospel. A concise statement of that gospel appears in Paul's letter to the Romans: *"If you confess with your lips that Jesus is Lord and believe in your heart that God raised him from the dead, you will be saved"* (10:9). The change from 'Messiah' to 'Lord' is possibly because some 15 years had passed since he ceased to preach that gospel and now, in the year 57, the two words were nearly synonymous.

This gospel of Messiah Jesus and his imminent return is what was preached everywhere for the first decade after the death and resurrection of Jesus. But where the message did not include justification by faith, it was simply a great delusion, a fantasy.

It is no surprise to us that they were deluded as to their preaching that God would send his Messiah soon. The amazing fact is that in the gracious purpose of God this faulty message resulted in so much true faith in Jesus as God's Messiah. It was correct only in that it was based on the resurrection (as in Romans 10:9), to which the twelve disciples were witnesses. What message could have been better suited to win many converts in Jerusalem?

Thus, again divine benevolence brings blessing out of human blunderings. But human blundering continues, so God continually works to repair the damage we cause. That necessary messianic community in Jerusalem did more damage later in our story, but again, God used that too, for the blessing of the body of Christ, God's people everywhere, and throughout the centuries.

On the basis of this message of the imminent return of Messiah, not only in Jerusalem, Judea, Samaria and Galilee but in a dozen Gentile cities messianic communities were planted, as far west as Berea. Even though the message was divinely unauthorized and incorrect, it brought into being many communities of faith in Messiah Jesus.

The Imminent Return Gospel must have sounded perilously close to sedition. Luke tells us (Acts 17) that at Thessalonica the unbelieving Jews gathered a rabble and *"dragged Jason and some of the brethren before the city authorities, crying, "These men who have turned the world upside down have come here also, and Jason has received them; and they are all acting against the decrees of Caesar, saying that there is another king, Jesus.""* (Acts 17:6-7) A formal charge of sedition would be dismissed when it was learned that the said Jesus had been crucified.

In Jerusalem the community of those 'Jesus Messianists' considered themselves nothing more than Jews. In fact, they probably thought of themselves as more correctly Jewish than those who refused to recognize Jesus as their Messiah. This goes for the twelve disciples as much as for any other believing Jew up to the time of the private meeting at Jerusalem that Paul writes of in Galatians 2. Peter's (and John's) agreement with Paul that Titus need not be circumcised would make him most unwelcome in Jerusalem. But we're getting ahead of ourselves.

The results of this first epoch's proclamation are –

1.   The witness of the disciples to the resurrection of Jesus was proclaimed with such power that thousands of Jews believed.
2.   Along with that vital message a gospel was also preached that Messiah would soon return to re-establish a Davidic kingdom. At least a dozen

> believing communities were founded through this "Good News."
>
> 3. Paul too preached this gospel but he, uniquely, did not require Gentiles to become Jews, i.e. be circumcised and conform to Jewish ritual. Paul's companions (Barnabas, and later Silas and Timothy) learned this law-free gospel from him.

Additional Observations

In the gospel message of such preaching as *"there is salvation in no one else, for there is no other name under heaven given among men by which we must be saved"* (Acts 4:12), what do the words 'salvation' and 'saved' mean? To answer that question we must consider what was offered in the message. What were the hearers of such a gospel invited to accept? Every Jew already knew the ideas of Messiah's restoration of the Davidic kingdom and the judgment of Israel's enemies. For each individual, 'salvation' meant inclusion in the kingdom; judgment would be the lot of all not 'saved.' The salvation and the judgment would follow close after Messiah's return; they would not be deferred to a future eternity. They would be made real and visible on the establishment of the kingdom here on earth.

The prayers of the earliest believers included *'maranatha,'* 'our Lord, come' (1 Cor 16:22), reflecting the almost universal belief that Messiah would come soon. After all, in their minds Messiah had no other function than to restore the kingdom to Israel, and inclusion in that would constitute their salvation.

One more item deserves mention. On the way to the northern Aegean area of Troas and Philippi, Paul met and circumcised the half-Jew, or incompletely Jewish, disciple Timothy. This was quite in keeping with his preaching of the imminent return of Messiah. The presence in his retinue of an 'incomplete' Jew would be an embarrassment in his preaching a Jewish gospel to Jews.

> The Jewish framework of the Christian movement is clear not only from the frequently reflected conviction of the disciples that they rightly worship in Temple (Acts 3:1, 21:26) and synagogue (Acts 6:9, 9:20, 13:14, 18:4), but also from the access which the Judaizers have to largely Gentile churches, which do not regard the presentation of the claims of legalistic Judaism as utterly alien to their own heritage as Christians. (Filson, *The NT Against its Environment*, 16 ftnt.)

We have now a complete story of the progress and success of a gospel of the imminent return of Messiah, all the way from Jerusalem to Pisidian Antioch and on to Berea, but a gospel of delusion, as many believers began to realize when year after year Messiah failed to return. The progress made was that of the inclusion of Gentiles into the faith community of God's people, plus being able to be in a right relationship with God without having to be circumcised or observe the ritual law of Moses.

Up to this point no believers in Jesus had ever heard of Christians or Christianity. What could the word Christianity have meant to them? Even the speech of Stephen had offered nothing; his merit was to point out the obstacles in Judaism to the future establishment of

Christianity, which offers salvation through Christ to all humans everywhere, in contrast to Judaism's Messiah for Jews and those Gentiles who were circumcised. In the above the term 'Messiah' is used to indicate the risen Jesus in the imminent return gospel, and the terms 'Christ' and 'Christian' are reserved for the universal gospel of the cross: "Christ died for our sins." As to the word 'Christianity' in the title of this piece, no alternative is available. The word church is avoided in connection with the communities which knew only the gospel of Messiah's imminent return.

Another point. Deuteronomy 21:23 says that one hanged on a tree is accursed. Paul was to deal with this later. Meantime, this Old Testament passage no doubt gave many Jews reason to reject a crucified Jesus as Messiah. However, our story is not of unbelievers.

> [Paul] does not say that a curse is an impossible attribution for the crucified Christ. Rather, he turns the passage around in a surprising way to make it a prophecy, showing that Christ had changed the curse so as to bring the blessing of Abraham to the Gentiles. (Segal, *Rebecca's Children*, 106.)

This is the story of the earliest gospel as far as the New Testament data takes us. The imminent return gospel, (which attached no value to Jesus' death), of being put right with God by faith in Messiah Jesus, and forgiveness of sins, reached as far as Thessalonica and Berea; the date: 42 AD or thereabouts, not as in the most widely held views. (This date appears in this book's Chronology).

To sum up briefly, the Gospel was:

1. Messiah has appeared, as evidenced by his Resurrection from among the dead
2. very soon he will return to establish his Kingdom
3. believers are put right with God through their faith and
4. their sins are forgiven.

The only surviving letter of Paul's from his 'imminent return of Messiah' period is that which we call Second Thessalonians, written, perhaps from Berea. (Arrangement of documents in compilations in ancient times was by length, not by when they were written.) Its concerns are thoroughly Jewish: the recent (AD 40) instruction of Caligula to erect a statue of himself in the temple at Jerusalem would have incensed one like Paul who still felt himself a Jew. Is "the man of lawlessness, taking his seat in the temple of God" (see 2 Thess 2:3-4) a veiled reference to Caligula? In the letter the God of the Jews is much like the Jehovah of the Old Testament, violent and vengeful, not at all like "the God and Father of our Lord Jesus Christ" of Paul's later letters, or even like "see that no one of you repays evil for evil" of First Thessalonians. Second Thessalonians is quite in line with the expectation of Messiah's setting up a Davidic kingdom, which is what Paul too expected. Then at Corinth everything changed, as the first phase of Paul's gospel preaching came to an end.

Study 3

The Beginning of the Gospel
(Philippians 4:15)

The Second Phase of Paul's Ministry

Paul's ministry entered its second phase after he left Macedonia. And he called this "the beginning of the gospel." Writing this near the end of his life, he looked back on his preaching of the imminent return as not a true gospel, in contrast with what henceforth he called "my gospel," that of "Christ and him crucified," the Christ who "died for our sins."

A Garbled Story

For the story of the first proclamation of the gospel in Corinth we have two sources, Paul's letters, and the book of Acts by Luke. In the latter there appears to be a deliberately garbled account; Luke seems to want his more perceptive readers to recognize that he is not giving a straightforward narrative. Luke tells us (Acts 18):

* Paul went to live and work with Aquila;
* he argued in the synagogue every sabbath, and persuaded Jews and Greeks;
* Paul was occupied with preaching, testifying to the Jews that the Messiah was Jesus;
* when they opposed and reviled him, he shook out his garments and said to them, *"Your blood be upon your heads! I am innocent. From now on I will go to the Gentiles."* (Acts 18:6)
* he left there and went to the house of a man named Titius Justus, a worshiper of God; his house was next door to the synagogue;
* Crispus, the ruler of the synagogue, believed in the Lord, together with all his household;
* many of the Corinthians hearing Paul believed and were baptized;
* And the Lord said to Paul one night in a vision, *"Do not be afraid, but speak and do not be silent;"* (Acts 18:9)
* the Lord said to Paul, *"I am with you, and no man shall attack you to harm you;"* (Acts 18:10)
* the Lord said to Paul, *"I have many people in this city."* (Acts 18:10)

These ten are as they appear in Luke's account. The sequence is all wrong. For instance, the Lord tells Paul to speak and not be silent after he has spoken for perhaps a week. And why the word, "Do not be afraid" to one who is never seen as fearful? Also, the promise that there would be many converts was given after many Corinthians had already believed.

Did Luke, a first-rate story teller, realize he was not telling a straightforward story, or did he have some purpose in giving these details so oddly? Why would he, apparently deliberately, have written such a bungled story? What was in his mind? Before answering the question we must see what Paul says. Collingwood wrote that all history is the history of thought, that the historian's task is to reconstruct what was in the minds of the people making the story and in the mind of the one writing. What was in Luke's mind as he wrote? And why so many details, at least fifteen? No other city was given nearly as much attention. There must have been something special about Corinth.

> The arrangement of this story shows some anom-
> alies. The incident of Paul's appearance before
> Gallio is inserted between the comment of verse
> 11 on the duration of Paul's stay at Corinth, which
> normally would have appeared at the story's end,
> and the mention of his departure without being
> connected with it. Also it is plain that a lacuna
> exists before the story of the vision as nothing is
> said of the possible risks which the apostle was
> running and made him think of leaving the town.
> The story would be much more coherent if verses
> 9-11 came after verse 17. The accusation of the Jews
> would have appeared such a threat to Paul that he
> would have thought of leaving the place. The rear-
> rangement may have been determined by a desire
> to play down the gravity of the incident. If this is
> the case then the appearance before Gallio took
> place not, as is customarily supposed, at the end
> of Paul's stay at Corinth but considerably earlier, at
> the time of his break with the synagogue. (Goguel,
> *The Birth of Christianity*, 21-22.)

So we cannot even claim without further ado, as is the habit of so many scholars today, that Luke only knew what he reported about the early period of Christianity. He certainly knew a good deal more than he put down; when he is silent about something, there are usually good reasons for it. Only by this strict limitation of his material can he 'put his heroes in the right perspective' (Hengel, *Acts & the History of Earliest Christianity*, 36.)

In his letter to the Thessalonians from Corinth not long after he arrived there Paul wrote *"our Lord Jesus Christ died for us."* (1 Thess 5:10)

From First Corinthians:

* Paul baptized Crispus Gaius, and the household of Stephanus;
* Christ sent him to preach the gospel;
* Then his remark: *"The word of the cross is folly;"* (1:18)
* *"it pleased God through the folly of what we preach to save those who believe."* (1:21) Also
* *"When I came to you, brethren, I did not come proclaiming to you the testimony of God in lofty words or wisdom. For I decided to know nothing among you except Jesus Christ and him crucified. And I was with you in weakness and in much fear and trembling; and my speech and my message were not in plausible words of wisdom, but in demonstration of the Spirit and of power."* (2:1-4)
* Much further on Paul states, You were the first to whom I preached that "Christ died for our sins" (15:3).
* *"I received from the Lord what I also delivered to you, that the Lord Jesus on the night when he was betrayed*

> took bread, and when he had given thanks, he broke it, and said, 'This is my body which is for you. Do this in remembrance of me.' In the same way also the cup, after supper, saying, 'This cup is the new covenant in my blood. Do this, as often as you drink it, in remembrance of me.' For as often as you eat this bread and drink the cup, you proclaim the Lord's death until he comes" (11:23-26).

*   *"I would have you know, brethren, that the gospel which was preached by me is not man's gospel. For I did not receive it from man, nor was I taught it, but it came through a revelation of Jesus Christ."* (Gal 1:11-12) This is consistent with what he tells the Corinthians.

Enough data is now available to reconstruct what was in Luke's mind when he penned this apparently bungled story. It hinges on the content of the visions Paul had, in one of which he was told not to be afraid, and to stop being silent. It seems Luke here wanted his readers to wonder: Paul afraid? Paul silent? Luke has so far presented Paul as totally fearless, as always eager to speak. It is always Paul who took the lead, even when with his senior, Barnabas. What did Barnabas ever say? It seems he never had a chance to say anything. Paul always jumped in ahead with something to say. What did his other companions, Silas and Timothy, ever say? Never a word from any of them; they seem never to have had an opportunity. And afraid? One who repeatedly went back into the synagogues where he so infuriated the Jews that five times he was flogged with the 39 stripes? Are afraid and silent proper words to use of such a man? Paul's quite uncharacteristic fear and silence, demand further explanation. That is to be found in Paul's letters.

Robert L. Greenhow

Luke had an over-riding purpose in writing – to publicize and promote Christianity. And it was highly successful as promotion and seems to have greatly furthered the reception of the gospel. In addition he had several subsidiary aims, one of which was to make Paul, his work and his letters widely known. It would hardly have been to the purpose to portray his hero as fearful, weak and trembling, afraid to preach his message. But this is exactly what Paul frankly writes was the case. Luke naturally felt he couldn't say such a thing of his hero. Evidently Luke also wanted to puzzle his readers about the early preaching of the gospel in Corinth, and point them to Paul's letters, especially those to the Corinthians, where the rest of the information could be found to solve the puzzle.

A plausible story of Paul at Corinth

With what is in Paul's letters, and Luke's information, a coherent and plausible story can now be told. The first item is his receiving the revelation "Christ died for our sins," along with some instruction that he was to proclaim this as God's gospel. The statement seems to have stunned him; he felt he couldn't preach such an outlandish message.

Other writers have stated:

> (Paul) stressed that element in the gospel for which current wisdom could have no place: what more abject spectacle of folly and helplessness could be imagined than a crucified man? A crucified deliverer was to Greeks an absurd contradiction in terms, just as to Jews a crucified Messiah was a

piece of scandalous blasphemy. (Bruce, *Apostle of the Free Spirit*, 253.)

Why a stumbling-block to the Jews? Because a crucified Messiah was a flat contradiction of Jewish convictions and hopes. The Messiah was to be the glorious vindicator of Israel and the Israelite ideal against the wicked cruelty and godlessness of the world-empires. A crucified Messiah was a Messiah defeated by the heathen empire, and that was a contradiction in terms. (Manson, *Studies in the Gospels & Epistles*, 22.)

(Jesus) was identified with his race as it lay under the judgment of a broken Law; and the form of his death proved the completeness of the identification. But once more his triumph over that death which spelled curse, meant triumph over the Law which imposed the curse and the deliverance of his people from its yoke. (Scott, *Christianity According to St Paul*, 40.)

Paul preached nothing for several days, fearing public ridicule. Then came the further divine message, "Don't keep silent; there is nothing to fear; and besides, I have many people in this city." With this implied promise of a true response from both Jews and Gentiles, he began his public preaching "with fear and trembling," but with many people responding in faith, "in a demonstration of the Spirit and of power." So was born the church in Corinth. (See Acts 18:9-10 and I Cor 2:4)

The "demonstration of the Spirit and of power" probably indicates that the first converts were immediately filled with the Holy Spirit and spoke in tongues. What other than such speaking could a "demonstration of the Spirit" have been? The pattern had always been that the first time a particular kind of audience accepted the gospel, their reception of the Holy Spirit was demonstrated, for the assurance of the preacher, that God was at work with him in the proclamation of the divine message.

This time it was not the audience, but the message itself that was entirely new. It is surely significant that the only church to which Paul wrote concerning tongues was at Corinth, and they were certainly familiar with tongues before he wrote about them.

Paul was himself converted from the earlier belief to the later by his own preaching, reluctantly and in fear and trembling, on witnessing the positive results of his foolish message, the conversion of many Corinthians, both Jews and Gentiles, and by seeing the "demonstration of the Spirit" in those converts speaking in tongues, proof to him that this was a powerful divine work. This conversion did not yet nullify his belief in an imminently returning Messiah. Paul could still write what we read in First Thessalonians, the clearest statement in the New Testament of that belief that Messiah would soon return, quite compatible with both "Christ died for our sins" and "Christ died for us." The combination is seen in *"our Lord Jesus Christ, who died for us so that whether we wake or sleep we might live with him."* (5:9-10) The "wake or sleep" refers back to 4:15 and its context.

It is an indication of Luke's skill that he gives us this information without compromising his story of Paul's triumphal march with the true gospel of Jesus Christ all the way west to Rome. Even in his imprisonment Paul manages to present the gospel to the highest dignities and authorities in the east, both Jew and Roman. Luke tones down but does not conceal the fact that Jerusalem remains steadfastly Jewish, for Jews only, right to the end, while Paul takes Christianity to the rest of the world.

Much has been made of the progress in Acts of the gospel from Jerusalem to Rome; this should be amplified by a more important progress from an illusory Jewish gospel of an imminently returning Messiah to a universal gospel of Christ crucified for our sins; from a deluded, 'wishful thinking' gospel of Messiah's imminent return to a heaven-sent gospel, incapable of being devised by any human, and in reality, from the standpoint of human reason, utter nonsense, but *"the power of God for salvation."* (Rom 1:16)

Paul's experience at Corinth had been foreshadowed by Peter's at Caesarea; he was converted by his own preaching. But Paul, unlike Peter, had preached reluctantly, not fully persuaded of the truth of what he was saying. On seeing "the power of God" using "the foolishness of God, wiser than men" to convert so many, he "decided to know nothing but Christ and him crucified." Never again did Paul fear to proclaim that message, or keep silent as to it.

Another revelation taught him the significance of Jesus' last meal with his disciples, the main parts of which he had probably heard from Peter, such as some of what Jesus had told them.

Now Paul has divine instructions (1 Cor 11:23) that this Supper is to be regularly celebrated as a proclamation of Christ's death –

In the Synoptics' (Matt 26:26-29; Mark 14:22-25; Luke 22:14-20) account of the last supper:

1. All report that Jesus said, when he took the bread, gave thanks and broke it, "This is my body."
2. All report that he also said, when he took the cup, "This is my blood which is poured out … "
3. All connect the blood with "the covenant" with the possible inclusion of 'new'.
4. Jesus referred to the meal as the passover, the defining ritual feast of Israel, complemented soon after the Exodus with the covenant, (Ex 24:7-8) ratified by blood. (Heb 9:18)
5. Jesus does not elaborate on the expression "my body".

Jesus here was implying that this was a new passover with a new covenant (Jer 31), ratified by his own blood. He is not explicit that he was the slain lamb of the passover, but Paul got the point and wrote that Jesus is our passover lamb. (1 Cor 5:7)

Neither Matthew nor Mark say anything about 'remembering' as part of what Jesus said during the meal. Luke says, "Do this in remembrance of me." This is in the Greek exactly the same as what Paul wrote, as quoted above. Luke evidently took this from Paul's copy of his letter to the Corinthians. It seems that its being a memorial or remembrance feast was part of the revelation from heaven, not a recollection of anything said at the last supper. Thus, if this is correct, there would be no basis for anyone thinking that believers in the early days had a ritual meal to remember the Lord's death. It was a new institution at Corinth.

The institution of this custom of remembering the Lord Jesus Christ at the Lord's table, was, in addition to being a feast of remembrance, a proclamation of the Lord's death. God intended that the Lord's Table be the focus of the weekly meeting of the church. The gatherings previously had no true focus, being simply synagogue style meetings of the new messianic communities for prayer, the reading of the scriptures and exhortations.

It is unlikely that this revelation came at the same time as "Christ died for our sins;" this was a message for Paul himself, that of the Lord's Supper was for the church of Corinth, which had not yet been founded. But it probably was received soon after Paul formed the new believers into a church. It was no doubt one of the "abundance of revelations" he was given.

As the passover was a memorial of Israel's deliverance from bondage, so the new Israel was to have both a memorial of deliverance from the bondage to sin, and a covenant, ratified by blood. Jesus probably did not count on the disciples to whom he was talking, to understand what has just been outlined, but he probably hoped that enough of them would report or record what he said, so that someone, like Paul, could receive and understand another revelation as to it, which is what happened.

The Lord's Supper was to be a time for true Christian table fellowship. The believers were to gather once a week for a common meal, with a loaf and a cup of wine the focus of everyone's attention. Sometime during the meal the loaf of bread, broken and given thanks for, was to be passed around for all to partake of; likewise the cup. (This is the picture given in First Corinthians, especially chapters 11 and 14.)

Robert L. Greenhow

> The sorts of activities in the meetings were also probably similar (to those in the synagogue), including scripture reading and interpretation, prayers, common meals, but in neither case the sacrifices that were characteristic in pagan cults. The Pauline meetings were also marked by prophecy, admonitions, the reading of apostolic letters, and by glossolalia and other phenomena of spirit possession. (Meeks, *The First Urban Christians*, 80.)

During or after the meal there would be singing, prayer, prophecy, reading of the scriptures, as Meeks says, words of edification etc. This fellowship meal was to be a replacement of the passover for the new Israel of God, but with a transformation from

* an annual Passover to a weekly (or oftener) meal and
* from a commemoration of deliverance from Egyptian bondage to a deliverance from sin and its power and from its ultimate penalty, and
* most important, from a ritual meal including animal meat, to a thankful remembrance of the death of Jesus Christ our Lord – Christ, our Passover Lamb has been sacrificed. (1 Cor 5:7)

By their meeting weekly in happy fellowship, a truly Christian community was established, the first local Christian church.

> Although rare in the ancient world, conversion was characteristic of Judaism and Christianity, as well as of some philosophical schools and mystery religions. The commitment of a convert differed from the usual religious "adherence" to certain formal

rites and rituals which were unique to each city. Most of these rites and formal pieties were merely civic rites, not demanding the kind of commitment that Judaism or Christianity found to be central to their way of life. (Segal, *Rebecca's Children*, 99.)

Paul, through the faithful discharge of his function as a herald of the gospel, had developed a consciousness which was new in history, that of a pastor, a man to whom it was a matter of life and death that his converts, his children in the faith, should be loyal to Christ and also to one another, and that they should progress in the knowledge and fine character which spring from truth. (Scott, *St Paul, The Man and the Teacher*, 64.)

The church "is the arena wherein God's reign is to be most fully at work, and it is the instrument through which God's reign is to be most adequately expressed to an alien world" … Faith in Christ is meant to be the basis for a life of expanded vision, sharpened sensitivities, moral courage, and active endeavor, not a substitute for thought or change. (Longenecker, *NT Social Ethics for Today*, 96.)

Summary of events at Corinth

1. Revelation that "Christ died for our sins" (15:3).
2. Revelation re Lord's Supper as remembrance and proclamation of Christ's death (11:23ff).
3. Instruction as to nature and character of the Church (13:1-30 + 10:15-17).

4. Instruction as to regular practice and procedure at Lord's Table (14:1+ 26-31).

5. Answers to various questions relating to conduct (7:1ff, 8:1ff, 16:1ff, all of which begin: "Now concerning ... ," referring to questions the Corinthians had asked in a letter, now lost. That they had also asked other questions is evident from the way Paul writes in various parts of his first extant letter.

6. Paul's response to news of disorders: indirectly, in the last four chapters of his second letter Paul leaves it to the Corinthians themselves to examine their own conduct, repent and correct it.

Now more by other commentators:

The early expectations of a triumphant return of Christ had not been fulfilled. His sufferings were not (as some at least had hoped) a mere transient phase of his work, quickly forgotten in the glory which followed. The difficulties therefore which the apostles met at the first preaching recorded in Acts had to be met in a new form. The apostles had shown that the death of Christ was no obstacle to His Messiahship in view of his resurrection and implied return. [Acts 2, 3, 5] (Westcott, *Epistle to Hebrews*, liv.)

To this end it is necessary to realize distinctly the sharp contrast between the early popular expectations of what Christianity should be, especially among Jewish converts, and what it proved to be. And it is necessary also to realize the incompleteness with which the significance of the Lord's sufferings was at first apprehended. (Ibid.)

As the word of God, the gospel is indeed a divine communication; and it includes facts, truths, and doctrines. However, if the gospel does no more than communicate facts and doctrines, it has been reduced to the level of human tradition. In the word, God communicates not only facts about redemption and truths about himself; God communicates himself, salvation, eternal life. The word of God is both the report about a redemptive event, and is itself a redemptive event, for in the word of the cross, the Crucified himself confronts men to communicate to them the benefits of his redeeming death.

> We may now draw certain conclusions about the Pauline concept of revelation. The focus of revelation is Jesus Christ. In the event in history of Jesus' life, death, resurrection and exaltation, God has revealed himself redemptively to men. (Ladd, "Revelation and Tradition in Paul", in Gasque & Martin, eds, *Apostolic History & the Gospel*, 227-228).

> The word of the cross has "foolishness" at its heart, and to remove this by making the cross reasonable is to deny its meaning. Against world wisdom with its self-assertion, the cross with its self-denial must ever seem foolish. (Stagg, *The Book of Acts*, 58.)

> This love will take no man's choice from him; for it is precisely his choice that it wants. But its will to lordship is inexhaustible and ultimately unendurable; the sinner must yield. God has exposed the strong right arm by which he has declared that he will curb the nations. And lo, it is pierced by nails, stained with blood, and riveted in impotence. Is it to us too an offense and foolishness? Yet this is

71

the authentic quality of love's omnipotence. 'The weakness of God is stronger than men' – than any man; for 'I, if I be lifted up from the earth, will draw all men unto myself'. (Robinson, *In the End God*, 133.)

Reason argues that because God is righteous, it is only the righteous who can be saved. "What reason cannot grasp, in the final analysis, is the sheer miracle of forgiveness." "There is nothing" said Forsyth, "which is such a surprise, such a permanent surprise and such a growing surprise to reason as grace." (Barry, *The Atonement*, 155.)

We must begin to recognize that a simple clear-cut pattern fails to be sensitive to the ambiguous and elusive character of the relationship between God and the evil in his creation. Atonement means a conviction that God has somehow dealt with evil, with sin, with rebellion. Perhaps the nearest we can get to expressing this is to say that on the cross, God in Christ entered into the suffering, the evil, and the sin of his world; he entered the darkness and transformed it into light, into blazing glory. He took responsibility for the existence of evil in his creation; he bore the pain of it and the guilt of it; he accepted its consequences into himself, and in his love reconciled his holiness to a sinful and corrupt humanity, justifying the ungodly, accepting man just as he is … . (Young, *Sacrifice and the Death of Christ*, 94.)

In [the book of] Hebrews Jewish sacrifices were rejected on principle, and the principle was an entirely new one … It was an assertion that Christ's sacrifice had replaced them. Sacrifice should no longer be offered by Christians, not because Christ's message was in conflict with the Old Testament revelation of the past, but because he had so fulfilled it as to make it meaningless. … The sacrificial system was not condemned but shown to be wanting; ultimately only the death of Christ fulfilled the purpose of the Law. Jewish sacrifices were to be rejected, not simply on negative critical grounds, (like Stephen's) but because of a new interpretation of sacrifice in the light of Christ's death on the cross. (Ibid., 50.)

For the Christian Jews, the author of the Epistle to the Hebrews gave one answer: The perfect priest, Christ, is also the final, perfect sacrifice, and the old cult is no longer needed. As to the polity of old Israel, the Christians held that it had lasted until the coming of the Messiah and ended with the crucifixion of Jesus and the Jews' rejection of Christ. The ruler's staff (Genesis 49:10) had finally departed from Judah. (Neusner, *From Politics to Piety*, 98.)

In Paul's view, the Messiah was pre-existent; a heavenly being, the Messiah became the man Jesus for the period of Jesus' earthly career. Unique to Paul, as compared with the abundance of utterances about the Messiah in Apocalyptic and Rabbinic literature, is his interpretation of the career of Jesus as related to sin and atonement. (Sandmel, *Judaism and Christian Beginnings*, 207.)

A man in union with the Christ is a new creation. Through the Christ, God had reconciled Paul to him, and had put on Paul the burden of reconciling other men to God. Paul accordingly, was an ambassador in the role of Christ. ... [Sandmel's note 46]: The idea appears to be that man, because of sinfulness, had become alienated from God. The death of the Christ, bringing atonement from sin, ended that alienation, thus becoming reconciliation. (Ibid., 326-7.)

Paul's accomplishment was that, more than anyone else, he transformed the new movement from one essentially Jewish into a Gentile movement free of all obligation to the scriptural laws. (Ibid., 334.)

The natural meaning is that Paul is speaking of a revelation. Some prefer to understand the phrase "received from the Lord" as meaning "received from church tradition." My own view is that Paul means revelation, not about the practice, but about its meaning. (Ibid., Note #29, on 1 Cor 11:23. 469.)

This Gospel says that in Christ God has acted as never before and with effective power to carry his purpose to climatic fulfillment, and that since this message, by its very nature and content, permits no neutrality, God's action in Christ calls for a response of faith and loyalty. (Filson, *New Testament Against its Environment*, 20.)

[Paul's] preaching to the Gentiles as well as to the Jews, and the defense his letters make of the truth and universality of the gospel, impress us so deeply that we often fail to see how hounded and hated he was. (Filson, *Three Crucial Decades*, 19.)

… a clear and authoritative word about the gracious action of the holy God, a theology in which the cross is the natural symbol of the seeking love of God and in which the resurrection is the interpreting focus of the triumphant Lordship of God. This message finds a true foundation and prelude in the Old Testament, but it cannot be set down as merely another statement of what is equally clear and effective in that earlier form. When God acts decisively he gives to those of faith a climactic revelation, in the light of which all else is to be interpreted and understood. Theology strictly understood finds its basic and constant material in the action and person of the God and Father of our Lord Jesus Christ. This is the New Testament presentation of God. It did not come from its environment. It is either an original human delusion, or a fresh, climactic revelation. (Filson, *New Testament Against its Environment*, 23.)

Paul's Work after Planting the Church at Corinth

Instructing the church at Corinth was the culmination of Paul's Aegean journey with the gospel. The group of believers at Thessalonica had already learned from Paul's letter that "Christ died for us." Though so similar to "Christ died for our sins," it is not at all foolish, and had ample precedent, like the Spartans who died at Thermopylae in defense of many Greeks. The Romans too had their heroes who had died for Rome.

Perhaps during the 18 months Paul spent at Corinth he had an opportunity to visit the Thessalonians briefly; now Paul wanted to teach them that "Christ died for our sins" and that 'more' which would establish them in their faith. Also to teach the church the proper way to remember the Lord at his Supper.

Similarly wherever numbers of believers of Paul's messianic gospel met regularly they needed to hear the new cross gospel from Paul himself. It is assumed that he taught all of them that "Christ died for our sins" and also all that he had taught the Corinthians. Thus they would become truly Christian churches. They would be transformed from mere synagogue-style messianic communities into true Christian fellowships gathering once a week for a common meal at which the Lord's Supper would be the focus of everyone's attention, and with singing, prayer, prophecy, reading of the scriptures, words of edification etc.

For the next ten years or so Paul wrote no letters. Probably he was fully occupied in studying the Scriptures, and pondering the implications of that mysteriously foolish but powerful message, "Christ died for our sins." But he was also busy evangelizing, in Crete as well as in north Galatia and elsewhere. In Acts this period is concealed between verses 11 and 12 of Chapter 18.

Now to consider the views of another commentator:

> The difference in form (between Jesus' and Paul's teaching) is so great as to preclude any suggestion

of quotation, while the correspondence of thought is too close to allow of independence. ... But the possible explanation of the phenomenon calls for attention here; ... we are confronted by a harmony which appears not only in the details of ethical teaching, but in the principles, and in the balance and emphasis with which they are brought to bear upon conduct. The Christian man as he is delineated by Paul is extraordinarily like the portrait of an ideal disciple as it may be constructed from the teaching of Jesus ... . (Scott, *Christianity According to St Paul*, 14.)

There in the Bible of the Greek-speaking Jews the word *'soteria'* had long ago established itself as a synonym for the complete fulfillment of Israel's hope in God. The content put into the word at different periods and by different men varied with the changing interpretations which were put upon man's highest good. It might mean no more than deliverance from impending danger to life or to liberty; it might mean no less than triumphant participation in the transcendent Kingdom of the Messiah. It might stand for something wholly corporate or national, or equally for something intensely personal and individual. But whatever the form of deliverance or the quality of privilege which it connoted, it was expected that God would vindicate his character ('show his righteousness') by sending 'salvation' to his people. The promises of the prophets, the prayers and aspirations of the psalmists alike had found in the word the highest expression of religious experience. (Ibid., 21.)

> [Jesus] was identified with his race as it lay under the judgment of a broken Law; and the form of his death proved the completeness of the identification. But once more his triumph over that death which spelled curse, meant triumph over the Law which imposed the curse and the deliverance of his people from its yoke. (Ibid., 40.)

The Traditional Understanding of the Early Gospel

> Here [1 Cor 15:3] was the Church's message from the date of its birth. **Christ died for our sins.** (Stewart, *A Man in Christ*, 288.)

> The gospel is that **Christ died for our sins**. ... That is exactly the gospel which was preached on the day of Pentecost. (Ironside, *Lectures on the Book of Acts*, 100.)

Those who say that "Christ died for our sins" was proclaimed from the earliest days maintain that First Corinthians 15:3 and 15:11 demonstrate this.

Others, writing on 1 Corinthians 15:3:

> "... first, not in reference to time; nor first to the Corinthians, which would not be historically true ... ." (Hodge, *First Epistle to the Corinthians*, 312.)

> "*en protois* cannot be masculine. It would be too obvious an exaggeration to rank the Corinthians

among the first to be reached by this Pauline tradition. We shall take *protois* as a neuter." (Héring, *First Epistle of Paul to Corinthians*, 158.)

«paredoka et parelabon (tradition récue et transmise) ont ici un sens si évidemment dégagé de toute espèce d'ambiguité, que cela nous a aidé à fixer celui de xi, 23.; ... il faut donc comprendre 'en tout premier lieu' comme premier enseignement.» (Allo, *Première Épitre aux Corinthiens*, 390.)

"The derivative nature of the gospel is stressed. Paul did not originate the message he passed on to them. It was what he had himself received... . 'First of all' is probably not concerned with time but with importance. "I put in the first place ... ". (Morris, *First Corinthians*, 205.)

"Paul's own adaptation of the Christian tradition, which he had received from his predecessors (1 Corinthians 11:23; 15:3) ... ". (Beker, *Heirs of Paul*, 124.)

So also Hans Conzlemann, Gaston Deluz, John Ruef, Leonard Goppelt, P. T. Forsyth, Gordon Fee and doubtless others.

C. K. Barrett leaves the question unanswered: "the ambiguity of the Greek *en protois* ... may indicate priority either in time or in importance – naturally the two may well coincide." (Barrett, *Commentary on 1 Corinthians*, 337.)

Both meanings, as Barrett suggests, are valid. The Corinthians were the first to hear that Christ died for our sins, and that truth is of the utmost importance.

The above authors maintain that the Greek words *'para-doka'* (received) and *'parelabon'* (handed on) both appearing in verse 3, both being used for the receiving and handing on of tradition, demonstrate that, no matter what Paul says elsewhere, his gospel did not originate with him, that others preached the same gospel that Paul goes on to outline in 15:3-8. To which the reply is –

"Christ died for our sins" is so foolish that no one could have thought it up, much less proclaimed it as Good News. It could only have come from above, as a divine revelation. And furthermore, Paul writes to the Corinthians "you were the first to whom I preached 'Christ died for our sins.'" (What Luke records of the first day of our era is that Peter explained what the people were witnessing – so many people speaking in tongues was the gift of the Spirit as foretold by the prophet Joel. Then Peter accused his hearers of murdering their Messiah.)

"Christ died for our sins" was foolish but not futile. Christ's death demonstrated the love of God, *"in that while we were yet sinners, Christ died for us"* (Rom 5: 8) and *"in Christ God was reconciling the world to himself."* (2 Cor 5:19)

As to when "Christ died for us" was first preached

> Many scholars have … concluded that the Cross did not have the central place in the gospel according to Jerusalem which it certainly had in the gospel according to Paul. (Caird, *The Apostolic Age*, 39.)

... in Acts the death of Christ tends to be treated negatively, as an unfortunate event which nevertheless, in view of the resurrection, need not be an obstacle to faith. (Barrett, *Luke the Historian*, 57.)

James Dunn in *Unity and Diversity in the New Testament*, (4.2) points out that the death of Jesus is frequently mentioned (Acts 2:23, 36; 3:13-15; 4:10; 5:30; 7:52; 10:39; 13:27-29) as a historical fact but is not interpreted as being "for us" or "for our sins".

In Aramaic-speaking Jewish Palestine, round about the year 30, could the notion of the universal representative atonement achieved by the death of the Messiah come into being at all? A number of counter-arguments are advanced against this possibility. (Hengel, *The Atonement*, 57.)

Every tradition must begin sometime, somewhere. Why should it not have been as Paul says, begun when given by the Lord, the only possible source of such foolishness, but a foolishness which the Holy Spirit used to save many Corinthians. We have noted that all the evidence is against that foolish message ever being taught in Jerusalem, where the believers continued on "yom kippur" (Day of Atonement) to practice another means of clearing their consciences of the guilt of sin, by continuing their forefathers' custom of offering animal sacrifices. Such had been done for centuries, why should it not continue? Nothing had been written by their prophets about Messiah dying for sins; why accept such folly and offensiveness? The prophets had always assigned another function to Messiah.

Well then, what of First Corinthians 15:11 – *"Whether then it was I or they, so we preach and so you believed."* Here Paul says that he and the original twelve preached the same message. This is no difficulty when it is recognized that there was originally another gospel, the gospel of the imminent return, based on the resurrection of Jesus.

Note how Paul separates the preaching of the cross from that of the resurrection. In the first chapters of First Corinthians he emphasizes the cross, and says not a word of the resurrection. In the 15th chapter he is arguing for the resurrection, and apart from verse 3 (where he could hardly avoid mention of Christ's death in an outline of his gospel), he says nothing of the cross. We have seen that for some years Paul preached a resurrection gospel; the imminent return of Messiah depends for its validity on the resurrection while his death is quite irrelevant. So Paul, recollecting his pre-Corinth days, recalls that as far as the resurrection is concerned, he and the twelve disciples all preached the same gospel.

Look now at what Paul writes: "Christ died for our sins." First we should recognize that a legitimate rendering of First Corinthians 15:3 is "You were the first to whom I preached that 'Christ died for our sins.'"

Those who insist that Paul derived his gospel from others, by their reading of the words *'paredoka'* (delivered) and *'parelabon'* (received) in First Corinthians 11:23 and 15:3, perhaps do not realize the seriousness of what they are doing. If they were right so were the Judaizers who harassed Paul's churches and Paul would have been making himself a liar. Indeed, he would have perjured himself, and that before God! He wrote, *"Before God I do not lie!"* (Gal 1:20)

If the Judaizers were right in claiming that Paul got his gospel from those before him, why would he take such a great risk as to deny it under oath? He would have known that they could easily get the names of those who told him, and he would be utterly discredited! None of Paul's detractors called his bluff when they could have easily done so. Paul's claim that his gospel was a revelation direct from the Lord himself, is quite convincing.

Establishing and instructing the church at Corinth was the high point of his Aegean journey with the gospel. It was the parting of the ways; this instruction was so different from all previous teaching, now outmoded. It was really the beginning of a new era, as Paul tells the Philippians. (4:15.)

Study 4

The Jerusalem Council

Nothing has yet been said about early disputes as to the preaching of the gospel or as to the believers' habits, other than the questioning of Peter's eating with Cornelius and those in Cornelius' house. However, many in the messianic community in Jerusalem vigorously opposed Paul's law-free message before he received his revelations at Corinth. Some of these followed Paul and in the churches he planted preached that it was necessary to be circumcised and practice the rules of Jewish daily life.

Paul was temporarily at Antioch, perhaps recuperating from one of his floggings; apparently it was his first visit there since his learning that "Christ died for our sins." He naturally taught the believers there this wonderful new message, also instituting at Antioch the Lord's Supper.

Then Peter too came to visit the church at Antioch, heard and presumably accepted the new message and joined in the table fellowship of the Lord's Supper.

It is probably in the setting of the visit to Antioch of the Jewish Christians who urged the circumcision

of Gentile converts that we should place the episode related by Paul in Galatians. 2:11-14. (Bruce,
New Testament History, 283.)

Bruce is not explicit that Peter had arrived in Antioch and
had already begun to eat with the Gentile converts before Bruce's "Jewish Christians" arrived and started their
Judaizing efforts, not only urging circumcision but reject-
ing table fellowship with Gentile believers. The episode of
Paul in Galatians 2:11-14 is that of his rebuking Peter for
yielding to the Judaizers' urgings and withdrawing from
table fellowship with the Gentile brothers. This was the
prelude to the Council of Jerusalem, as told in Acts 15, and
Paul's private meeting with the Jerusalem three, as related
in Galatians 2.

"Conflict between Paul the apostle to the Greeks,
and the narrow Jewish Christianity of the original
disciples was the clue to the history of the apostolic
age." (Ellis quoting Baur in his article "Paul" in the
New Bible Dictionary, 947.)

To Baur Galatians 2 and Acts 15 tell of the crucial episode of
the 'conflict.' Understanding what happened at Jerusalem
illuminates many passages in the New Testament. Paul's
effort to preserve "the truth of the gospel" (Galatians 2:5
& 14) was vital. Without his prompt and decisive action,
Christianity would have reverted to being a mere sect of
Judaism.

The thorny question: how can both the stories in Galatians
2 and in Acts 15 be right? This has consumed very much
time and attention. In 1845 F. C. Baur argued that the meeting in Jerusalem of Galatians 2 could not possibly be that

of Acts 15. T. W. Manson said Baur's argument was "unanswered and unanswerable." For well over a century and a half debate, ignoring Baur, has continued with no consensus. A possible solution: there was more than one meeting.

The background –

As already noted, Paul was temporarily at Antioch, when "certain men came from James" (Galatians 2:12), Judaizers from Jerusalem, "those who were unsettling" the church (Galatians 5:12). They did so by teaching that the Gentile believers must be circumcised and that Jewish believers must not eat with those Gentile believers who were uncircumcised. At a gathering of the church for the fellowship meal, Peter withdrew, followed by Barnabas and others, "fearing the circumcision party". (Gal 2:12)

Understandably, Paul was furious. Even when Peter had known only the Jewish kingdom gospel of Messiah's imminent return, he had eaten with the gentile Cornelius and his friends, and had successfully defended his doing so against accusations of un-Jewish conduct in Jerusalem. Now, when that increasingly dubious gospel has been supplemented by the universal gospel of the cross, how could Peter refuse to eat with his Gentile brothers and sisters! Paul rebuked Peter before the whole church....

Though neither Paul nor Luke records it, Peter (and Barnabas) accepted Paul's rebuke, repented and resumed their practicing full table fellowship. Otherwise how could Barnabas have sided with Paul against the circumcision of Titus (Galatians 2), and how could Peter have argued (Acts 15) against *"putting a yoke on the neck [of the Gentile believers] which neither our fathers nor we have been able to bear?"*

Robert L. Greenhow

(Acts 15:10). Precedent had already been set when Peter had eaten with those Gentiles who had received the gift of the Holy Spirit in Cornelius' house at Caesarea (Acts 10).

In Acts 15:2 Luke wants to refer to the episode at Antioch of Galatians 2 when Paul rebuked Peter for withdrawing from table fellowship with Gentile believers, as well as the matter of circumcising Gentiles. He writes, there was "no small dissension and debate"; this could include both. As a result a delegation was sent from Antioch to Jerusalem. Paul says, "I went up by revelation." (Gal 2:2)

Acts 15:4 reads– "they were welcomed by the church … " A welcome could be extended by a church only as it was gathered together. But then after that welcome by the church, "the apostles and elders were gathered together to consider this matter [circumcision and keeping the Law of Moses]." (15:6)

(Just as Solomon was the reputed author of Proverbs, and David author of the Psalms, so Moses was the purported giver of all laws. [Then as now, these all were time-honored literary fictions.] Thus the Jews who clamored for the Gentile converts to conform to their dietary and other rules attributed these rules to Moses.)

"Apostles and elders" implies a second and smaller group; it made all the important decisions.

Paul writes of a private meeting, not only private, but secret, because Paul realized that if both he and the uncircumcised Titus were known to be in the area, the circumcision party might be stirred into some unpleasant activity.

The Private Meeting

At the private meeting Peter, James and John, the 'pillars', represented the Jerusalem congregation, and from Antioch, Paul, Barnabas and Titus. Paul and Barnabas told what God had done through them among the Gentiles (see Acts 15:12); God's activity included the winning of Titus. Perhaps at this point the matter of Titus being circumcised was raised by James and John. Paul rejected that and argument followed. James and John tried to persuade Paul that Titus should be circumcised, unsuccessfully. Paul was adamant: Titus is not to be circumcised. The vigor of Paul's language and his evident agitation while writing Galatians 2 indicate that the meeting must have been a lively one. Paul no doubt anticipated that the meeting would be lively, which is reason enough for him to have insisted that it not be public. He knew that the temper of the Jerusalem community was such that they would hotly demand Titus' circumcision if the topic was raised in the congregation.

Paul says, *"I laid before them ... the gospel which I preach among the Gentiles, lest somehow I should be running or had run in vain."* (Gal 2:2) That 'gospel' could only be that of Christ crucified. Not only was this gospel – "Christ died for our sins" – and its implications so convincingly presented that John, at least, was convinced, (Peter had already been persuaded at Antioch) but the Jerusalem group agreed that Titus need not be circumcised. It may be that the universality of the appeal of that gospel is what won the day.

Paul also raised the matter of the Judaizers' troubling his churches with their demands that Paul's converts Judaize. The Jerusalem three eventually acknowledged that they need not; furthermore, there was mutual agreement: Paul would go to the Gentiles, the Jerusalem three to the 'circumcision.' However, both Peter and John apparently left Jerusalem and Judea. Hans Dieter Betz, without considering any of the above, says that as a consequence of this meeting, Peter had to flee from Jerusalem. (*Galations*, 82) No doubt for Betz it was enough that Peter agreed to the non-circumcision of Titus.

Another thing: Paul used the words "running or had run in vain." The 'running' here has nothing to do with the preaching of the gospel or the teaching of the believers. Nor could it have been anything to do with his own faith in Christ, his own salvation. It was his constant struggle against those Judaizers who would have brought the churches he had planted "into bondage" to law. Had he been struggling against them for years in vain? Was he even now at Jerusalem in this meeting possibly running in vain? If he could not persuade the 'pillars' in Jerusalem to restrain the Judaizers, he would have failed; he would have been running in vain. However, in the end Paul won his case. Having succeeded in "preserving the truth of the gospel," Paul and Titus apparently then left for Antioch.

> … Weiss … holds that Paul was not present at the meeting recorded in Acts 15. (Davies, *Paul and Rabbinic Judaism*, 118.)

> In Galatians 2:2 the words immediately following 'according to revelation' are explanatory of it: 'I went up according to revelation and I laid before them the gospel which I was preaching among the Gentiles.' The fact that Paul laid before them the gospel he had been preaching strongly suggests that until this

time they had not actually heard from him about the uniqueness of his gospel. It seems most unlikely that Paul would have made a special trip to lay out before the apostles the details of a gospel which they already knew. (Howard, *Paul: Crisis in Galatia*, 38.)

The Apostles and Elders Meeting

Luke sometimes takes liberties with minor details of the historical reality, to preserve the optimistic tone of his story of the gospel's progress toward Rome, with a minimum of trouble, of which there was, unfortunately, very much, even after Paul's apparent success.

Part of Luke's ideal history is the combining of the three meetings into one, indicated in 15:12, where the reporting of the success of the gospel among the Gentiles is historically that of the Galatians 2 private meeting, as told above.

In Luke's report of the meeting of the congregation, when some of the Pharisee party demanded the circumcision of Gentile converts, that demand was quieted when Peter very commendably said, *"Brethren, you know that in the early days God made choice among you, that by my mouth the Gentiles should hear the word of the gospel and believe. And God who knows the heart bore witness to them, giving them the Holy Spirit just as he did to us; and he made no distinction between us and them, but cleansed their hearts by faith. Now therefore why do you make trial of God by putting a yoke upon the neck of the disciples which neither our fathers nor we have been able to bear? But we believe that we shall be saved through the grace of the Lord Jesus, just as they will."* (Acts 15:7-11)

What Peter said at the Jerusalem Council, that putting "a yoke on the neck (of the Gentile believers) which neither we nor our fathers have been able to bear," sounds like Paul. Quite possibly, in addition to what Paul wrote in Galatians 2:14, he said something very much like that in rebuking Peter at Antioch. Peter seems to have been able to accept a rebuke, and in this case, even to learn from it, and use much the same language at the Council, if this conjecture is near the truth.

Thus Paul's two points both carried the day: 1) Gentile converts need not be circumcised, and 2) table fellowship (the matter of 'kosher' food and kosher eaters) cannot be denied to any Gentile brothers in Christ. But face is saved for Jerusalem in that James, the leading brother of the Jerusalem congregation, pronounces the final decision and proposes the council's decree, which mentions only matters of eating and drinking. It is a win – win – win conclusion. However, the Jerusalem Judaizers simply did not consider themselves bound by it. (The above is a way to see the historical reality, as distinct from Luke's story.)

This analysis of Paul's theology and personality has been necessary to illuminate the significance of the Jerusalem Council and its aftermath in the whole history of Christianity. Behind the controversy over circumcision and the attitude to gentile converts a whole range of the deepest issues was at stake. Nor did the suggested compromise of James and Peter work. It was based on a ruling from Leviticus which provided for the entertainment of strangers and allowed a certain relaxation of the law. This was precisely the kind of misplaced casuistry which Paul thought ruinous to

Jesus' message. Paul made no attempt to put it (the decree) into operation. ... But equally Paul's opponents did not abide by the apostolic ruling. ... For Paul, it was literally a matter of life and death, and his own writings make no attempt to hide its gravity and acrimony. (Johnson, *A History of Christianity*, 40.)

The Pharisees who believed insisted that the Gentiles should be circumcised when they became Christians. They regarded Christ's religion as a mere extension of Judaism and considered that in converting the Gentiles the great object was to increase the observers of the Law of Moses. (Foakes-Jackson, *The History of the Christian Church*, 36.)

Jesus' brother James ... was in a fair way to make the Christian movement, in Jerusalem at least, little more than a new form of Pharisaism, when he encountered the strong opposition of the apostle Paul, who had been a thorough Pharisee in his youth and had seen the hollowness of it. (Goodspeed, *A Life of Jesus*, 36.)

So long as James lived, Jerusalem was the centre of the Church and the Christians there aspired to the role of an holy remnant leavening and guiding the Jewish people in the short intervening period that remained before the end of the age. (Frend, *The Early Church*, 38.)

Paul's great insight contained in these words (Israel of God) unique in the New Testament, shows his recognition of the major role that Israel in its long story had to play in the preparation for the gospel. Christianity is no new thing. It is the culmination both of God's choice of Abraham as the founding father of the People of God, and of the faith and moral standards of the Old Testament. (Neil, *Galatians*, 88.)

Indeed, Luke was right. Jews, Christians, and pagans of the empire attacked Paul. Had he been permanently discredited, the future of Christianity would have been different from what it was. But in fact the book of Acts became canonical, and in harmony with Luke's aim Paul was accepted as the great missionary and theologian of the church. This meant that the gospel of grace, the universality of the gospel, and the ethical integrity of Spirit-led life in faith were protected in a way which otherwise would have been impossible. The apologetic of Luke on behalf of Paul was of crucial importance for the future understanding of the gospel and for the future life of the church (Filson, *Three Crucial Decades*, 21.)

... as far as (Luke) is concerned, the legitimation of the mission to the Gentiles is virtually Peter's last work (Acts 15). This represents a clear choice in favor of the 'thirteenth witness' and proves that (Luke), for all the theological problems which he presents to the Paulinism of modern theology, was a decided Paulinist himself, albeit of a very distinctive kind ... the proclamation of the risen Lord begun by the twelve apostles is brought to consummation ... It is also quite consistent with Luke's point of view – seeing that he does not mention Paul's letters and probably did not even know of them – that the authentic letters of Paul should form the centerpiece of the so-called 'apostolic writings' in the New Testament canon... Presumably Luke, without knowing it, made a decisive contribution towards giving Paul's work this unique position in the early church (Hengel, *Acts & the History of Earliest Christianity*, 125.)

The church down to the present day owes more to (Luke's) work than theologians are usually wont to allow. (Ibid., 126.)

Revision of Acts 18:22

Luke was not with Paul for this part of his story, and the sources Luke was dependent on may not have been wholly reliable. For whatever reason, some re-arrangement is needed because from Ephesus Paul went to Antioch before he went to Jerusalem.

According to the text, Acts 18:22-23 reads, after he set sail from Ephesus – *When he had landed at Caesarea, he went up and greeted the church, and then went down to Antioch. After spending some time there he departed and went from place to place through the region of Galatia and Phrygia, strengthening all the disciples.*

This story, as shown by the parenthetical additions, requires something like –

When he had landed at Antioch and after spending some time there (seeing Peter come, hear and, presumably, accept Paul's gospel of the cross, followed by the rebuking incident), he went up and greeted the church (at Jerusalem, had his private meeting) then went back to Antioch. After spending some time there (during which he wrote to the Galatians) he departed and went from place to place through the region of Galatia and Phrygia, strengthening all the disciples.

* * * * *

Just when in Paul's career did he and Barnabas, and Titus, go to Jerusalem to protest against the Judaizers' activities? It was probably soon after his second missionary journey. Even though Luke knew from Paul's letter to the Galatians that Paul had been teaching or preaching for at least 14 years, he had good reason to make it seem as if it was after the first journey. Furthermore Luke's story up to Acts 15 allows no such prolonged activity.

These reasons included:

1. reiterated statements close together that the gospel was to go to the Gentiles: Acts 14:27, 15:3, 15:7;
2. Peter's making a highly commendable statement just prior to his final exit from Luke's story;
3. Peter's immediate replacement by Paul;
4. that this should seem to be the commencement of Paul's independent gospel activity.

For those who protest against the suggestion that Luke knowingly put the story of the Jerusalem Council out of place, consider the differing state of affairs in his day and ours. Today our lives are governed by timepieces including the calendar. Radio and TV are precise to the second. In Luke's day there were no timepieces, not even printed calendars. Our daily lives are governed by the week (though our records and documents are dated by the month). In the Greco-Roman world, there was no week. To us whose lives are precisely controlled by the calendar and timepieces, their state of affairs is scarcely credible. Time in all its aspects imposes a tyranny over our minds of which we are usually unaware. Try to imagine life today, with people daily going to work or school, as they did too, without clocks or watches, without weeks, nor calendars, nor numbered years. Documents were dated as, in "the 51st year of the reign of Elizabeth 2, in the third month, on the 2nd day following the ides." Their attitude to time and the sequence of events must have been vastly different from ours, and much more casual.

Luke says nothing of Titus' being at Jerusalem as early as it is in Paul's account. It is virtually impossible; Paul had not yet visited Corinth, and it is only in connection with Corinth and Crete that Titus is spoken of. After Paul's second missionary journey it fits well.

Luke included material about Paul's private meeting and the public council in one story showing the reasons for both as well as their outcome. Writing at a later time when no one was much interested in the affair, Luke probably felt it mattered little whether the story was of one meeting or more than one.

(The rebuking incident at Antioch must have been prior to the private meeting at Jerusalem; Paul's eagerness to get the collection under way, together with his longing to go to Rome, would have kept him from setting up residence in Antioch after he had agreed, at the private meeting, to "remember the poor.")

When Luke wrote Acts the issue of whether or not the Gentile believers had to be circumcised had ceased to exist. No one cared about it, apart from the Jerusalem church, now in Pella, which had put itself outside the stream of church history. As long as his readers were left with an accurate general impression of the story of the early church, Luke could 'idealize' his story, even to the point of ignoring chronology, if and when by so doing he could emphasize important features. Furthermore, no historian in those days paid strict attention to chronology.

> J. A. T. Robinson says, (*Redating the New Testament*, 36.), It is when we come to tie up the Acts story with Paul's own statements in Galatians 1-2 that the real difficulties begin. There Paul relates two visits to Jerusalem – and two only – to make contact with the apostles. At this point we must give absolute priority to Paul's own account, not merely because he is writing in the first person, whereas Luke is at this stage clearly dependent on sources (and can be shown to be chronologically unreliable), but because Paul is speaking on oath (Galatians 1:20) and any slip or dissimulation on his part would have played into the hands of his opponents. Indeed we may say that the statements of Galatians 1-2 are the most trustworthy historical statements in the entire New Testament.

Robinson's "real difficulties" have been removed, as we have seen, and the chronological 'unreliabilities' explained.

Paul's success in "preserving the truth of the gospel," that is, that the gospel is as much for the Gentiles as for the Jews, was no trivial matter. If it had not been preserved at that time, all the Christian churches would have degenerated into Jewish synagogues, Christianity would have disappeared and Christianized western culture could never have developed.

> Whatever reservations the twelve apostles and the conservative Jerusalem Christians may have had, and however reluctant they may have been to face up to the issue, it was the unwavering belief of Paul, held with passionate conviction, that Christ had broken down the barrier between Jews and Gentiles and that there must be no second-class citizens with his church. ... for them [the conservative Jerusalem Christians] circumcision was still an obligation, the Temple of Jerusalem and all that went on in it was still the focus of their worship. (Neil, *Galatians*, 10.)

From beginning to end, Jewishness is a hindrance to the gospel in Luke's account. From the beginning to the end of Paul's career Jewishness is a hindrance to his proclamation of his gospel, or at least to the fully free reception of it. Constantly Jewishness is made a requirement by Jerusalem and/or its emissaries, official or unofficial, so that Gentile converts are made anxious lest their 'salvation' be invalid or not genuine without law works, including circumcision. The conflict was put to rest only by the destruction of Jerusalem, too late to give Paul any respite.

In all the discussion at the private meeting and at the Council, there is no mention of any work of Christ; he is mentioned only in the expression, "saved through the grace of the Lord Jesus". Apart from this everything is entirely Jewish. Towards the end of the book, in Jerusalem the elders tell Paul, *"You see, brother, how many thousands there are among the Jews of those who have believed; they are all zealous for the law."* (Acts 21:20.) What kind of Christianity is it that would ignore Christ, and glory in its totally Jewish observance of the law of Moses?

> Luke sees Jerusalem as the place of God's decisive acts and the place where witness is borne to them. (Lampe, *Luke & the Church of Jerusalem*, 15.)

> In this final narrative of Acts Jerusalem and its spiritual leaders lose their opportunity to be the focus and centre of the Christian movement. In other words, these closing chapters attest both the potential continuing importance and the actual dispensability of Jerusalem and its temple for the Christian church … As was true in the ministry of Jesus, Jerusalem cannot be ignored; the gospel must be preached there; if it is ready to accept its opportunity and responsibility, it will continue to be the centre and focus of the Christian church; the gospel will continue to go out from there; it will lose its primacy only by its own decision, and particularly the decision of its leaders, not to accept the gospel. (Filson, "The Journey Motif in Luke-Acts" in Gasque & Martin, eds, *Apostolic History and the Gospel*, 74.)

> Luke in this final third of Acts is presenting the lost opportunity which Jerusalem had and the

essential transfer of the centre of the church from Jerusalem to Rome. (Ibid., 75.)

The earliest Christians had greater difficulty than the Essenes in freeing themselves from the Temple … . (Johnson, *A History of Christianity*, 18.)

The attitude of so many men, fostered by the Jerusalem community as a whole, is incompatible with a faith in a crucified Christ, a Christ who died for our sins. It is quite compatible with faith in a risen Jesus, demonstrated by his resurrection from the dead to be Israel's imminently returning Messiah. But the two faiths cannot be combined in such a way as to retain such aggressive and hostile Jewishness as was shown by the Judaizers who caused the division in the church at Antioch.

The realization that eight of Jesus' twelve disciples were among those who rejected or ignored the gospel may seem saddening to us; Luke had ample opportunity to talk with them, and would certainly have recorded any positive word of their going abroad with the gospel if there had been such. And they had been told "that repentance and forgiveness of sins should be preached in my name to all nations, beginning from Jerusalem. You are witnesses of these things."

Those who believed the gospel, – Peter at Antioch and John at Paul's private meeting – did so rather late in their lives, in 52 AD or thereabouts. If when Jesus chose them they were young men, – probably in their twenties as traditionally assumed – they would be more than forty in 52.

Peter wrote "to the exiles of the Dispersion" and names five provinces in Asia Minor, so it is assumed that he evangelized that area. Silvanus was Peter's amanuensis; perhaps he was the same man as Paul's Silas. If he was, he was able to give Peter some of Paul's thoughts. In any case at several points in Peter's first letter a similarity of thought can be seen.

John was unusually observant as shown by his noting 1) numbers: 46 years to build the temple; 5 porticoes of the Bethzatha pool where the sick man had been ill 38 years, 153 fish but net not torn; 2) real conversations, as Jesus with the woman at the well, Jesus and Nicodemus, Jesus and Peter – questions, as to Peter loving Jesus. (There are no such conversations in the Synoptics.)

John was a thinker, and probably took notes of the above – probably when Jesus was with them – likely in a diary, along with his own thoughts.

John's Gospel is unique also in another respect: he puts his many comments in with his story so closely that sometimes it is difficult to distinguish them. However that may be, we are thankful for his Gospel.

The Explanatory Power of the New History

The postulate of an early gospel of an imminent return of Messiah Jesus explains many things which are puzzling if instead, "Christ died for our sins" was proclaimed very soon after the first Pentecost Day. Consider the following:

1. The new hypothesis explains why, in spite of Jesus' clear instructions to take his offer of forgiveness to the ends of the earth, none of the twelve disciples did that. Their firm belief in his very soon return had deafened them to his instructions; they wanted to be close to the seat of power on his return to this earth.

2. It explains why the primitive elements of preaching listed in Hebrews 6:1-2 include repentance, ablutions, laying on of hands, the resurrection of the dead and eternal judgment, but nothing about the death of Jesus. The list doesn't even mention him. All of the topics listed are features of Jewish doctrine.

3. Paul's letter, 2 Thessalonians, is the only surviving letter from his "Imminent Return of Messiah" period. There is nothing in it about the cross of Christ, having been written before Paul was given the revelation that "Christ died for our sins." But there is much about the coming of Messiah and of his warfare against his enemies. These Studies show why this letter resembles nothing else from Paul: all the others follow that revelation. (There is thus no reason for denying that it is Pauline.)

4. These Studies show why Luke excluded from Acts any mention of love; neither *agape* nor *phileo* appear, either in noun or verb form. From beginning to end of Acts, the believing community of Jerusalem demonstrated no love, on any occasion.

5. They also show why Luke excluded from his story any thought of reconciliation except once, in telling of Moses attempting to reconcile two Jews; significantly, the word is not in the Old Testament story. Luke seems to be emphasizing that in Jerusalem, the dominant faith community knew nothing of reconciliation. Those who eagerly awaited the return of Messiah, far from being reconciled to their enemies, were to fight and defeat them. The faith community of Jerusalem was to the end inhospitable to the gospel of the cross, the gospel of reconciliation. Paul's gracious and costly attempt to reconcile the Jerusalem faith community to the Gentile communities was spurned. So was he; during his two year confinement in Caesarea the Jerusalem community ignored him and were indifferent to his plight.

6. It explains Paul writing, "if I still preach circumcision … ." (Gal 5:11) As already said, Paul preached the imminent return gospel and that was a Jewish gospel. So, looking back to his pre-Corinth days, he thought of himself as having preached, in contrast to Christianity, Judaism, for which a synonym was circumcision. (cf Gal 2:7, 8, 9)

7. "the beginning of the gospel, after I left Macedonia." (Philippians 4:15) This has been perplexing to those who thought only of the gospel of the cross from Pentecost on. But these words are in complete accord with the sequence of events we have been seeing. Paul did not preach Christ crucified until after he had left Macedonia; he began to preach the cross of Christ at Corinth.

8. It explains why Paul felt that the gospel of the cross, "my gospel," was peculiarly his, and with good reason. It had been given by the Lord as a revelation to him alone, and to no one else.

9. Those who hold the conventional or traditional hypothesis contradict Paul even when he most strongly insists that his gospel came to him by revelation. (Gal 1:11-12) These Studies have Paul telling nothing but the facts of his own experiences.

10. The charge that Paul's practice was inconsistent, in that he circumcised Timothy but refused circumcision to Titus, is empty. Paul circumcised Timothy during his "imminent return of Messiah" period; he practiced what he preached, namely 'circumcision' – Judaism. Circumcising Titus would contradict the new law-free gospel of the cross of Christ, a gospel coming from the mouth of God himself and accepting no assistance from anyone as to their own salvation and redemption. This gospel is of God in Christ reconciling the world to himself... not counting their offenses and misdeeds against them. (2 Cor 5:19)

11. Paul's statement "I laid before them the gospel I preach among the Gentiles" (Galatians 2) is very strange if, as many insist, Paul got his gospel from those before him, specifically from Peter and others, like Barnabas. But if John and James had never before known exactly what it was Paul preached, there is nothing odd about it. So Paul wanted to be sure they knew what he preached, and he laid the cross gospel before them. Indeed, only a clear

laying out of the cross gospel could show why Titus must not be circumcised.

12. That it was Paul's own gospel, the cross gospel, that he explained to them is clear. Both John and James did know what Paul preached when he was preaching the imminent return gospel, even his law-free version of it. They must also have known that the 'zealous-for-the-law' Judaizers were vigorously contradicting his law-free doctrine.

13. This demonstrates that the need Paul felt for the private meeting must have been because he not only wanted to show why he could not permit Titus to be circumcised, but also because he knew they, as well as the Gentiles, needed to know his cross gospel for their own highest spiritual welfare. Note too that Paul went up to Jerusalem "by revelation." The Holy Spirit was in it all, and wanted God's apostles to be fully enlightened.

14. The postulate of a gospel of an imminent return of Messiah Jesus – the Gospel of Glory – allows for the conversion of numerous Jews without their ever hearing that "Christ died for our sins." What they believed was the testimony of the apostles that Jesus had risen from the dead; that demonstrates that he was God's Messiah. Paul gives the essence of that gospel in Romans 10:9, in which the death or cross of Christ is not mentioned.

15. An imminent return gospel shows how thousands of believers in Jesus in Jerusalem could still live their lives as though they had never heard that

"Christ died for our sins." How could it have happened that that was proclaimed publicly and repeatedly with no protest from the temple authorities or anyone else that such a proposition was utter folly? How could believers in Jesus as their Savior from the power and the penalty of sin continue to be zealous for the law of Moses, including attendance at the annual Day of Atonement (Yom Kippur) ritual for the covering of the past year's sins? Were all of those thousands totally blind to the truths presented in the Letter to the Hebrews as to the futility of those animals still being sacrificed? Furthermore, how could any who truly believed that "Christ died for our sins" be opposed to the proclamation of that message to the rest of the world?

16. The canonical documents known as the General Letters of James and Jude were evidently produced in Jerusalem for the Jewish believing community. On the assumption that "Christ died for our sins" was believed by all in that community, how can it be that those letters say nothing about the death or resurrection of Jesus, or even about his words, attitude, and activities?

17. The latter part of Acts shows the thousands of believers in Jerusalem living and worshipping exactly like their unbelieving co-religionists, and as their grandparents had done before Jesus had been born. How is it possible for believers that "Christ died for our sins" could have their lives, conduct and habits unaffected in the slightest by that momentous event?

Commentary

The Undercurrent in Acts

The incomprehension, revealed in all the gospels, of the twelve disciples as to Jesus' mission and teaching continues in Acts, and eventually spreads to infect the whole large community of believers in Jerusalem, though Luke presents the facts in such an optimistic or favorable light that a surface reading of the book fails to reveal anything adverse or unusual.

The disciples' incomprehension consisted in their inability to conceive of Messiah in any other terms than those of conquering hero, vanquisher of the Roman armies and restorer of the Davidic empire. So they gave no room in their minds to the idea of Jesus being crucified, even with the promise of resurrection soon after. It just didn't make sense. They were incapable of seeing a spiritual dimension in the promises and prophecies of their Bible, though the way was clearly shown to a non-literal way of reading those writings. For instance, Jeremiah's saying that they were uncircumcised in heart can have meaning only spiritually. And how could God's laws be written on people's hearts except spiritually?

So Jesus and his disciples remained at cross purposes. His teaching made no sense to them at all. When his predictions came true and he was taken, judged, condemned and crucified, they were utterly bewildered.

But they did not scatter, disillusioned, and go their own ways, returning to Galilee; they continued to stick together, even though they had lost the main force that had held them together, namely, Jesus' charisma. This is in itself strong evidence of that great charisma, in which his love for them was the chief element. But with him gone, they had little reason for meeting together, though they apparently continued to do so.

Then he reappeared, unmistakably himself, and their dejection turned to joy. What they should have done is to say something like, "We were all wrong in not paying attention to your saying that you must be crucified and rise again. Tell us why all that was necessary. We can't make any sense out of it. Why did you have to suffer as you did?" But no, that was not in their thoughts, but rather, "Now will you restore the kingdom to Israel?" (See Acts 1:6) He and they were still at cross purposes, and that fact is the basis of the undercurrent, evident (to the keenest eyes) all through Acts, of disunity, disharmony, and spiritual darkness, the focal point of which was Jerusalem.

The first action taken by the disciples underscores their total lack of understanding. They evidently saw something in the symbolic number twelve which, with the defection of Judas, was no longer true of themselves. It was necessary to restore that number, as it indicated that they were the core of the new Israel. But their subsequent habits showed that they were firmly entrenched in the old Israel; more than ever before, attending the temple and making it the focus of their thought: *"They were all together in Solomon's portico"*. (Acts 5:12) Note the strong contrast with Jesus' attitude to the temple. To be the real kernel of the new Israel required obedience to Jesus' instructions to scatter to the ends of the earth proclaiming repentance and forgiveness in Jesus' name. For this they had the necessary qualification. They were witnesses to his resurrection; Jesus had conquered death and they could testify to the truth of that. But Luke presents the facts in such a way that his story glows with optimism, and close study alone reveals the undercurrent.

The elucidation of that undercurrent all through Acts is the theme of this chapter.

During forty days of appearances and talking together, the sum of Jesus' message was that in a few days the twelve would be empowered by the Holy Spirit to go to the end of the earth as witnesses to his resurrection. The implication is that the content of their preaching was to be that recorded at the end of Luke's Gospel: repentance and forgiveness. Apparently their minds were so full of their own ideas that nothing of what Jesus told them sunk in; they had other thoughts entirely, expressed in their question, "Will you now restore the kingdom to Israel?" Again, his answer seems not to have registered, as the end of Acts shows them still in Jerusalem waiting for the restoration of the kingdom, and having done nothing in accordance with Jesus' instructions.

Luke's story is about the doing of the divine will and plan by others than the twelve, though Peter and John are shown as having a minor part, in confirming the results of Philip's evangelizing of Samaria. But even here, in response to Simon's request, Peter first acts as a judge condemning Simon to perish, then urging repentance with the possibility of forgiveness. But Jesus had said nothing as to forgiveness as a possibility but as the assured result of repentance. Back in Jerusalem Luke's surface story is rosy: thousands of converts, including a large number of priests. Luke never suggests that there is anything odd about the continued attendance at the temple of these thousands, or about these priests continuing to serve in the temple engaged in their sacrificing duties. After all, they thought that when Messiah had restored the kingdom, the temple activities would continue as Moses and Solomon had prescribed them.

That the disciples took in nothing of Jesus' meaning or purpose is evident. In the incident of Ananias and Sapphira Peter took the stance of judge. If Peter had remembered how gently and lovingly the risen Jesus had dealt with him privately in his repeated question to Peter as to Peter's love for Jesus, and Jesus' personal commission to Peter to feed Jesus' sheep, would his words to Ananias have been different? Can we imagine Jesus himself dealing with Ananias as Peter did? (See John 21:15-17)

But if the twelve ignore the Lord's instructions, God will find other instruments to do his work, not in or through the temple but in a Greek-speaking synagogue. That all is not well comes to light through favoritism and complaints regarding the daily ration distribution. Isn't some sin evident either in the neglect of the Greek-speaking widows or in the complaining? Why did Peter and the twelve ignore such sin yet focus on Ananias' deceit?

However, seven deacons are appointed, though they are not shown acting as such, but as teachers and preachers. The first named is Stephen and attention centers on him, his message and martyrdom. This is a turning point in Luke's story.

The accusation against Stephen relates to the temple, "this place," and the customs delivered by Moses. The distaste of the twelve for Stephen and his teaching is made obvious by their absence. Stephen is a free-lance; if he gets himself into trouble with his wild ideas, that is his own lookout. The twelve will not risk defending him, or even daring to appear at his trial before the council. Of course, Luke is silent as to all this; he leaves the reader to detect the undercurrent by himself, and to figure out attitudes as much by his silences as by his words. The Jerusalem community of believers makes itself irrelevant henceforth in Luke's story of the progress of the gospel.

The accusation against Stephen was regarding "this place," the temple in Jerusalem. The temple has been important in the disciples' activities as reported by Luke, in spite of Jesus' confrontations with the temple authorities, his 'cleansing' of it and his prediction of its demolition. Henceforward it should have had no significance for his disciples. Jerusalem was to be merely the source from which the gospel was to go to the ends of the earth in the power of the Holy Spirit. Inasmuch as the twelve were intent on remaining in Jerusalem with its temple, presumably because that is where they expected the imminently returning Messiah to establish his capital, God used others, prompted no doubt by Stephen's influence, to take the gospel to other places.

Since the accusation against Stephen revolved around "this place" Stephen ignores it in his defense, the longest speech in Acts. He mentions many other places where God worked and studiously ignores Jerusalem and its temple, until the very end when he quotes Isaiah 66 to suggest that the temple ought never to have been rebuilt. Whether or not Jesus may have had the same thought, he certainly acted in the temple as though the authorities were usurpers. Nothing in his words suggests that he thought the temple had any proper function other than as a place of prayer. True worship needed no temple, according to Jesus. Had rumors about his words (John 4:21) reached Stephen?

Following Stephen's death Philip and others take the gospel to Samaria and other places, and Peter finds himself in Caesarea in the house of Cornelius who has had a vision and a message. *"So I sent to you at once, and you have been kind enough to come. Now we are all here present in the sight of God, to hear what you have been commanded by the Lord."* (Acts 10:33)

This was a lesson for Peter fully as much as for Cornelius. He professes to have learned the lesson, that "God shows no partiality," and that Gentiles as well as Jews are acceptable to God. The pity is that Peter ignored the lesson and the God-given opportunity to take the gospel aggressively to other pagan Gentiles, or at least to other 'God-fearers' among the Gentiles.

Instead Peter even eventually forgot the lesson and later allowed his Jewishness to get the upper hand again at Antioch, and yielded to the demands that the Jewish believers not eat with the Gentile believers.

Back in Jerusalem after Cornelius' conversion Peter successfully defended his conduct, but an ominous note is sounded by Luke, in that the "circumcision party" has formed. Although silenced on this first occasion, this party gained the upper hand and made Jerusalem the permanent stronghold of Jewishness, discord and vigorous opposition to the true gospel. This of course is gleaned from other parts of the New Testament; until the council at Jerusalem Luke is silent about it, though fully aware of it all.

Peter now is displaced as the missionary to the Gentiles, presumably because he showed no intention to pass through the door he had opened.

In his place stands Paul who eagerly and zealously evangelized the pagan Gentile world, with his home base at Antioch where Stephen's disciples had first included Gentiles among those seen as a proper audience for the gospel, and where an *ekklésia* of both Jews and Gentiles was founded, without any requirement that the latter be circumcised. Luke is not explicit on this point; he leaves it to us to understand this, as well as that table fellowship is freely practiced. Luke has already mentioned, in the Cornelius episode, that it was unlawful for a Jew to eat with a Gentile. Happily, at Antioch Jewishness was not an issue. The believers acted together simply as brothers and sisters without regard to racial origin. This would seem to be the beginning of the fulfillment of God's promise to Abraham that through him all the families of the earth would be blessed. For 17 years from the date of Paul's conversion the circumcision party made no open move against this happy state of affairs in Antioch.

At Samaria Peter had said something that indicated that he had not fully understood Jesus' words about repentance and forgiveness, if he indeed had harbored them in his mind. His statement as to the "possibility" of forgiveness indicates a limited understanding, already dubious in the Ananias episode.

It is not to be expected that anyone in these early days should have thought or acted according to the full revelation of the doctrines of the cross as given, for instance in the letter to the Colossians. However, Jesus had anticipated what is included in those doctrines by his instructions to proclaim repentance and forgiveness. Jesus qualified or limited forgiveness in no way. And if the forgiveness is true there is no way it can be limited or restricted. Forgiveness is absolute, as is grace.

From Paul's letter to the Galatians we learn that, some years later, Paul was back at his home base, Antioch, for an extended period when Peter came for a visit. At first he joined in with the Antioch fellowship, participating in the church's activities, including table fellowship. That meant eating with Gentile believers, just as he had done in Cornelius' house. Then certain men came "from James," which here is taken to mean that they were emissaries of the Jerusalem congregation. "Fearing the circumcision party" Peter withdrew from table fellowship, evidently making excuses that persuaded other Jewish believers including Barnabas to follow him in withdrawing, effectively splitting the *ekklésia*. Paul's indignation was roused and he publicly rebuked Peter for such action, showing that such action was a denial of the truth of the gospel.

Luke tells us nothing of the above, but does give another angle. He says that these men from Jerusalem were announcing, with the authority of Jerusalem, that the Gentile believers must be circumcised or they could not be saved. Undoubtedly this also provoked Paul into, as Luke puts it, "no small dissension and debate." Here the undercurrent rises to the surface just long enough to give rise to the Jerusalem council, in which Peter redeems himself by coming out in favor of Christian liberty, and in which James ignores the issue of circumcision (apparently along with everyone else) and proposes issuing a rather innocuous decree. This was done; the undercurrent resumes its invisibility.

From the long term perspective Luke does not falsify the results and does not unduly publicize Jerusalem's shame in favoring Moses' law over Christian liberty. In the long run Jerusalem was irrelevant (along with its insistence on circumcision), seeing that the twelve refused to follow Jesus' instructions, and instead took up permanent residence in Jerusalem. They left it to Paul and others to evangelize the world, and actively tried to oppose his gospel, preaching Judaism (and circumcision) as the true gospel, until the destruction of Jerusalem and its temple rendered their activities futile.

When Paul and his companions on his final eastward voyage arrived at Tyre, the believers "through Spirit told Paul not to go to Jerusalem." (See Acts 21:4) This is one of the last evidences of the undercurrent. This is soon followed by the acted parable of Agabus, with the same message, another piece of evidence. Evidently the hostility of the Jerusalem community towards Paul was widely known. The council some years previously had done nothing to diminish this, in spite of its professedly irenic outcome.

The final instances of the undercurrent are on Paul's last visit to Jerusalem, when those delegated to bring the fund collected presented it. The attitude of the elders to what was brought and to those who brought it, including Paul, must have been so grievously insulting and humiliating, that Luke has no alternative but to say nothing about the fund for the poor in Jerusalem.

Then after Paul had been induced to join four others in the discharge of a vow, he was accused of defiling the temple, seized and imprisoned, taken to Caesarea and held there for two years. As far as we can tell, the community of believers in Jerusalem did nothing to aid Paul, simply ignoring him and his plight.

Legalism dies hard. Law is popular: "Do this and you will live." In contrast, grace is unpopular and poorly understood; it is too simple: "Accept God's offer of eternal life; it's free, no strings attached." The first century antipathy of LAW towards grace remains strong two millennia later. "The law was given by Moses; grace and truth came by Jesus Christ."

In providing us with the evidence for the undercurrent Luke is true to the spirit of the Bible as a whole, showing the struggle between the carnal and the spiritual, the old man and the new man, between law and grace, the mortal and the immortal, the perishable and the imperishable. It is the principle enunciated by Paul in First Corinthians 15.42-50. It began with Cain slaying Abel, and ends with

Jesus' resurrection and the victory of the Spirit over the flesh, and Death vanquished by Life.

Luke Writing Acts

The book of Acts contains abundant evidence that when Luke decided to compose it, he was faced with an acute dilemma. Most readers never detect this evidence, but read the book as Luke wanted the general public to read it, a seamless story of the triumphant progress of the gospel of the risen Messiah Jesus from Jerusalem to Rome, with his great hero Paul unobtrusively taking the place of the original protagonist Peter who silently disappears from view.

The evidence is largely negative. Arguments from silence are usually weak, except when the silence is surprising or uncharacteristic, and calls for explanation. The most glaring is the exclusion of the words for love: *agape* and *phileo*, though Luke uses these freely in his Gospel. Though Acts is the only book with any claim to be a post-resurrection history of early Christianity it says nothing of Paul's rebuking Peter at Antioch, or of the temporary division of the church at Antioch, or of Paul's private meeting with James, Peter and John. There is not a word about Paul's letters, nor of his great collection of funds for the poor at Jerusalem even though Luke lists Paul's several travel companions representing the churches that had contributed to the fund. There is no mention of the hostility of the believing community in Jerusalem towards Paul, nor of Jerusalem's Judaizing emissaries who harassed his Gentile churches, other than "some men came down from Judea and were teaching" the need for circumcision (Acts 15:1).

When Luke reports the zeal of the Jerusalem believers for the Law of Moses he does it so skillfully that the ordinary reader sees it as something positive, whereas it actually indicates Jerusalem's antagonism to Paul's gospel.

Luke knew that the actual history of the first three decades after the passion of Jesus was a stormy one, characterized by strong hostility on the part of the messianic community in Jerusalem towards Paul, but in the interests of Christianity and its promotion Luke keeps the hostility in the background. The antagonism of Jerusalem toward Paul is shown in Paul's letters in which he writes of the constant efforts of its emissaries to disrupt or undo his work among the mainly Gentile churches he founded. Luke wanted the more studious readers to notice and understand much more than appears on the surface. Two features are especially noteworthy.

First, that the story summarized above is a sorry, loveless one is evidenced by Luke's exclusion, already noted, of the Greek words for love. Yet *agape* is the supreme characteristic of the gospel of Jesus, the gospel of God. And the word *agape* appears in every other New Testament document, though Luke couldn't have known that. The other common Greek word *phileo* also does not occur in Acts.

Second, the Jerusalem gospel of Messiah's imminent return is a loveless gospel. This is amply demonstrated by the actively hostile attitude of the messianic community in Jerusalem towards Paul and his churches throughout his active career and beyond it.

The Jerusalem community did not reciprocate the love that Paul had for his kinsmen the Jews, and there is nothing to show that the love of the original eleven for their Master was shared by the main body of the congregation. The Jerusalem *ekklésia* was based on a loveless gospel, the appeal of which was to the carnal man and his national pride and supremicism, but God graciously accepted this along with faith in the risen Messiah Jesus.

Luke's evident aims were that Acts, along with his Gospel, should promote Christianity and its story of Jesus and his servants, and that it would serve to introduce Paul where he was not known. Less evident is his hope that people would read his letters. In fact, Acts did promote both the collection and preservation of Paul's letters, and Christianity itself. His undercover aim was that the careful student would be able through his story, read alongside Paul's letters, to learn what actually happened. For instance, the letter to the Galatians tells of the incident at Antioch when Paul publicly rebuked Peter, and, I believe, successfully so in that Peter resumed his habit of eating with any believer, Jew or Gentile. The same letter tells of the private meeting of Paul, Barnabas and Titus with James, Peter and John, just before the meeting of the Jerusalem Council of Acts 15.

Another of Luke's aims was to publicize the historic connection between his Gospel and the letters of Paul who was Luke's 'father in the faith'; he wanted to make Paul and his Cross Gospel as widely known as possible. He wanted to publicize Paul's practice of taking advantage of Judaism's privileged status as a legitimized religion under the protection of Roman law. Consequently he names several officials, Sergius Paulus, Gallio, Claudius Lysias, Felix, Festus, the centurion Julius, Publius of Malta, all of whom except possibly Gallio looked favorably on Paul.

Luke relates incidents where those who mistreated him or were about to do so had to back-track. He thus shows the principal emissary of Christianity moving in the highest political circles.

Eminent Christian scholars date Luke's compiling of Acts to AD 68-69 or thereabouts, after the flight of the Jerusalem *ekklésia* to Pella and before the destruction of Jerusalem in AD 70. If we accept that dating, when Luke was producing Acts circumstances had completely changed from what they had been on the first notable Day of Pentecost. The *ekklésia* of Jerusalem, having fled to Pella no longer had any credibility or authority. The Jewish war (66-70) had begun with no realistic hope of driving the Romans from the land; inevitably the destruction of the temple loomed ahead. James had been executed in 62 by the high priest in the temporary absence of a Roman procurator at Caesarea, and James' brother Jude had replaced him as the leader of the community. The Jewish hope (and gospel) of an imminent return of Messiah Jesus had faded; it no longer had any appeal or force as a gospel message. Paul's distinctly Christian gospel of Christ and him crucified was the only gospel and it was being widely proclaimed. The imminent return message was even being forgotten.

The Jerusalem community of believers in Messiah Jesus had cut themselves off from ready contact with other messianic communities by relocating in a remote region across the Jordan. No other congregation seemed interested in perpetuating their antagonism towards Paul or their attempts at Judaizing his churches. In these very greatly changed circumstances at the time he was compiling Acts it is quite possible that Luke judged that there was no one now much interested in the early disputes over Jewishness.

He was free to seem to change, or even to actually change details in relating the only important public dispute, that at the Council of Jerusalem, provided that he faithfully reported what was said that had permanent important force, such as what Peter said in 15:8-11.

* * * * *

Luke's dilemma as to presenting the gospels must now have our attention. Luke's omission of any clear statement of Paul's gospel in Acts has elicited various explanations. I differ from all of them and offer another, as well as an explanation of why Luke gives us no clear statement of the first gospel.

A plausible reconstruction of Luke's thought is, "If I give a clear statement of the original message as everyone preached it, at some future time someone might want to revive it, seeing it was so successful at the beginning." (In fact, several times through the intervening centuries messianic 'imminent return' gospels have been persuasively preached, sometimes with catastrophic consequences.)

Again, very possibly Luke thought: "If I give a plain presentation of Paul's gospel, too many people would think that it was the only gospel ever preached. And I can't present both gospels; God could then be accused of having his servants first preaching a gospel and then changing his mind and giving Paul a second message. The solution in this dilemma is not to include either gospel stated clearly. My sources contain material which I can present as a hint as to what the first gospel was. (Acts 1:6; 3:20) Furthermore I myself heard Paul state his gospel; I can abbreviate that

123

Robert L. Greenhow

and write just enough (Acts 20:28) to show that I know what he preached."

One notable passage in Acts (10:36-43) includes no mention of anything approaching "Christ died for our sins," nor of Messiah's imminent return. It is simply a brief summary of what we have in the four Gospels plus Peter's (or Luke's?) conclusion: believers in Jesus receive forgiveness of sins through his name. This is true, Luke implies, whether the belief is in response to this or that gospel. For the reader's convenience here is that notable passage:

"You know the word which he sent to Israel, preaching good news of peace by Jesus Christ (he is Lord of all), the word which was proclaimed throughout all Judea, beginning from Galilee after the baptism which John preached: how God anointed Jesus of Nazareth with the Holy Spirit and with power; how he went about doing good and healing all that were oppressed by the devil, for God was with him. And we are witnesses to all that he did both in the country of the Jews and in Jerusalem. They put him to death by hanging him on a tree; but God raised him on the third day and made him manifest; not to all the people but to us who were chosen by God as witnesses, who ate and drank with him after he rose from the dead. And he commanded us to preach to the people, and to testify that he is the one ordained by God to be judge of the living and the dead. To him all the prophets bear witness that every one who believes in him receives forgiveness of sins through his name."

It is reasonable to suppose that Luke wanted some clear expression of a saving gospel in his book, without clearly stating Paul's gospel of the cross. This passage admirably fits this specification.

Speaking in Tongues

In the absence of a convincing and clear doctrine of inspiration, is there any way of being assured that any particular writer or piece of writing reflects the mind of God or that God intended us to have it substantially as it exists in the New Testament? I find a pattern of incidents which give me confidence that Luke tells of these incidents accurately and naively. By that I mean that he had no intention to convince us of his veracity or of the truth of his story; he simply was an honest story-teller, quite possibly unaware of the pattern. I feel much like Blunt probably felt in writing his *Undesigned Coincidences,* which he claims demonstrate the trustworthiness of the authors.

It is almost impossible that Luke could have invented the relevant stories. He repeats them as the eye-witnesses gave them to him. It is likewise almost impossible that the participants in the events 'forced' or faked what happened: the stories of the gift of the Holy Spirit on those occasions when it resulted in the spontaneous "speaking in tongues."

At the outset of this chapter I offer some remarks about such speaking. First, Jesus is not recorded as having ever done anything to result in anyone speaking in tongues. Inasmuch as he was full of the Spirit, there seems to have been no need for anyone else to have the Spirit in addition. But he promised after he had permanently parted from them that they would be given the Holy Spirit. But he said nothing about receiving any ability to speak in tongues. The gift of the Holy Spirit was to be a 'baptism', an initiation into a new entity. In addition, this baptism was to bring a new element into themselves.

Second, there was a distinctly new feature in each incident in which the gift of the Holy Spirit was accompanied by speaking in tongues. This new feature will be noted as we come to consider each incident. Several times it was a distinct class of people, members of that class, viewed from a religious perspective, not having yet received the Holy Spirit. But there are other kinds of newness.

Third, those who spoke in tongues must have been surprised to find themselves speaking in tongues, something none of them had ever done before. It could never have been done by prearrangement. Not only the speakers, but those who brought the gospel to them must also have been surprised to see and hear these people suddenly speaking in tongues.

Fourth, it was always a group, never a single individual, who received the gift of the Holy Spirit accompanied by the spontaneous and simultaneous speaking in tongues. In each case, those who thus spoke in tongues knew each other, and would thus know which among his/her acquaintances had had an experience like their own. There would thus be a strong bond established among the new believers, a tremendous asset in the founding of a new church.

Fifth, nothing of what anyone said is recorded verbatim; they simply spoke of the wonderful deeds of God. In other words, no new revelation was ever given, no doctrine promulgated. As to permanent results, the use of tongues seems almost pointless.

What the divine purpose is assumed to be, will appear later. As miracle, it is certainly low-key; it accomplished nothing, no healing, nothing produced like bread or wine, no change in the weather, no change in the bodies of those who thus spoke. These all resulted from Jesus' miracles. The only thing permanent in the incidents of speaking in tongues is that it gave those who thus spoke an experience that they probably never forgot. They knew that they had been given the Holy Spirit. And they knew that a considerable number of their acquaintances had had a like experience which bound them together into a special fellowship.

Sixth, Luke records no repetition of anyone speaking in tongues a second time, nor does he say anything to suggest that they did.

Luke once, I believe, intends us to infer from his language that the gift of the Holy Spirit was accompanied by the new believers speaking in tongues. Similarly, on two occasions Paul intends the recipients of his letters to remember the experience they had, of speaking in tongues, as evidence that they had received the Holy Spirit.

All of the above is by way of preparation, or background. Now to consider each event as Luke records it.

The first incident (Acts 2) was on the feast of Pentecost when the Holy Spirit was given to the approximately 120 believers gathered in the upper room, presumably in John Mark's parents' house where the twelve ate "the last supper". Something caused them to go outside where passersby from places remote from Palestine, people who spoke languages other than Aramaic heard them extolling God in their own tongues and naturally were amazed. A huge crowd gathered, presumably at some large open square to hear Peter preach. He finished by accusing his hearers of

Robert L. Greenhow

murdering Jesus their Messiah who was now risen from the dead, as he, Peter, and the other disciples, could testify. Alarmed, they asked what they should do and were told to repent of their crime and they would not only be forgiven but also receive the Holy Spirit. No mention however, is made of them speaking in tongues.

The question arises, what was the point of them being given the ability to speak in languages they had never used before? What was the divine purpose in so enabling them, miraculously, to speak on this one occasion only? The answer is found in the preceding chapter, in Jesus' prediction of their receiving the Holy Spirit. *"Before many days you shall be baptized with the Holy Spirit."* ... *you shall receive power when the Holy Spirit has come upon you; and you shall be my witnesses in Jerusalem and in all Judea and Samaria and to the end of the earth."* (Acts 1: 5-8) But why would they be sent to the end of the earth where their Aramaic or Greek would not be understood? Was not the power given by the Holy Spirit the ability to speak the languages of the peoples wherever they went with the gospel of forgiveness? Even if only the men among the 120 went, there would have been enough to evangelize the whole known earth!

The great tragedy, along with all the confusion and conflict caused by Jerusalem, of the early non-evangelizing of the earth was due to the refusal of the twelve to spread out from Jerusalem for at least fifteen years. They were the most credible witnesses to Jesus' resurrection though there were others, such as the 500 plus in Galilee, but these were not commissioned to be witnesses nor were they told to go to the ends of the earth with the message of repentance and divine forgiveness. Who can tell what blessing might have been bestowed on the nations if the twelve had been obedient to the Lord's instructions

The second time that the gift of the Holy Spirit was accompanied by the ability to speak in tongues was when Philip preached in Samaria and many professed to believe. (Acts 8) When Peter and John came, they prayed that these new converts might receive the Holy Spirit. Luke says nothing openly about anyone speaking in tongues, but Simon the sorcerer saw that the Holy Spirit was given. How is the reception of the gift of the Holy Spirit seen? Does anybody now ever see the Holy Spirit given? Are there any reports of the Holy Spirit's being visibly given? How would Simon see the Holy Spirit being given? The only way he could see it was by the recipients visibly speaking in tongues, and Peter and John were there to attest that this is what they had experienced on the day of Pentecost when they had themselves received the Holy Spirit.

Possibly there was a reason why the Samaritans did not get the Holy Spirit when they believed the message of Jesus the Messiah as preached by Philip. God had a lesson for Peter and John that Philip didn't need. This lesson was that the conversion of Samaritans was in the mind and purpose of God: Peter and John had explicitly been instructed to take the message of the risen Jesus to the Samaritans. That they had failed to do so merited a rebuke. But neither Peter nor John give any indication of any lesson learned or rebuke taken. But before I judge them too easily or harshly, I must ask myself, Have I learned all the lessons God has been teaching me, or recognized every rebuke he has administered?

The third episode occurred in Cornelius' house in Caesarea where he had invited relatives and friends whom he knew to be God-fearers like himself. (Acts 10) Soon after Peter began to speak of Jesus, the Holy Spirit came on all these pious Gentiles and they began to speak in tongues. This was another lesson for Peter; God was teaching him that those who were not Jews were nevertheless objects of God's love, grace and salvation. Peter seemed at the time to have learned the lesson; he even stated it thus: *"Truly I perceive that God shows no partiality."* (Acts 10:34) Furthermore he stayed overnight in Cornelius' house and ate with him contrary to the Jews' current oral law (though nothing in the Old Testament forbids such table fellowship).

Instead of taking this incident as a prod to begin leading the twelve out of Jerusalem to zealously evangelize the world Peter seems to have regarded this as an abnormal event, not to be repeated; certainly it was not to be thought of as normative in the minds of Peter and the rest of the twelve. If Peter had considered then what he expressed years later at the Council of Jerusalem, that God had chosen him to open a door of faith to the Gentiles, he might have applied the lesson to himself and to his own future career. Or if he had thought of Philip, on his way to Caesarea where he made his home, he might have realized that Philip was just as competent to preach to Cornelius; why did God intervene and use such exceptional methods as Peter's rooftop vision and Cornelius' angelic visitor and message, if not to teach Peter that he was God's chosen one to open a door of faith to the Gentiles.

Is this relevant to Cornelius' (along with his guests') speaking in tongues? I see their speaking in tongues as an essential part in the lesson God was teaching Peter.

When he was summoned to account for his un-Jewish conduct, it was the fact that the Holy Spirit had been bestowed
on the Gentiles that silenced the circumcision party. How
would Peter have known, whether still at Caesarea or
back in Jerusalem, that the Gentiles had received the Holy
Spirit without those Gentiles spontaneously speaking in
tongues?

Another feature is worthy of note. In the course of his
narrative of going to Cornelius' house, when these Gentiles
were given the Holy Spirit, "Then I remembered the word
of the Lord, how he said, 'John baptized with water, but
you will be baptized with the Holy Spirit'." On the day
of Pentecost Peter remembered the prophecy of Joel, but
not the promise of the Lord Jesus. To no one of the 120,
apparently, was their speaking in tongues regarded as the
promised baptism of the Holy Spirit. It was in Cornelius'
house that that realization came at last to Peter.

The point here is not that the coming of the Holy Spirit is
termed a baptism, but that the disciples had paid so little
attention to the words of Jesus. Even in remembering what
Peter did remember, he didn't remember the really important part. Here, more or less unwillingly, in the house of a
Gentile who had just been baptized with the Holy Spirit,
Peter suddenly remembers that his own similar reception
of the Spirit was promised by Jesus – *"you shall receive power
when the Holy Spirit has come upon you; and you shall be my
witnesses in Jerusalem and in all Judea and Samaria and to the
end of the earth."* (Acts 1:8) – and he doesn't recall why he
himself had been given the Holy Spirit: to authorize and
empower him to preach Jesus' gospel of forgiveness to the
Gentiles, like Cornelius! Even sadder in Peter's story is

that for years to come he still thinks of himself as having received a commission to preach to the Jews (Gal 2:7).

The next episode of speaking in tongues is not so named by either Luke or Paul. I make the inference from both the situation and Paul's words. At Corinth Paul was given a new revelation, a new message which he regarded as both utterly foolish and offensive, so he didn't immediately obey the instruction to preach it, but remained silent. He was afraid to proclaim such a message, nonsense to Greeks and scandalous to Jews. So the Lord graciously gave him another threefold order and message: 1) don't be afraid; 2) stop being silent; 3) "I have many people in this city." Paul writes that it was with fear and trembling that he obeyed and preached what he still regarded as foolish. I venture to think that he was amazed at the response, so many of the Corinthians believed, as the Lord had promised. He may also have been surprised that they also spontaneously spoke in tongues! In all of his preaching previously, though it was very productive preaching, there is no mention of his audience ever speaking in tongues. Why do I say that the Corinthians did?

Paul wrote to the Corinthians, reminding them of when he preached to them, and when they believed, of "the demonstration of the Spirit and of power." (1 Cor 2:4) What phenomenon is better so described than that of speaking in tongues? Paul was reluctant to proclaim the new message; what better lesson for teaching Paul that the new message was a divine message than the spontaneous speaking in tongues by those who believed the message? How better to convince Paul that the fulfilling of the promise of a rich harvest was divinely guaranteed than by the empowering of the believers to simultaneously and spontaneously speak in tongues? In view of Paul's previous reluctance, fear and silence, plus his thought that the divinely revealed message was foolish and offensive, the new sight of his hearers suddenly speaking in tongues would have been a gracious gift from God to Paul as well as a rebuke not to argue with God.

To no other church did Paul ever mention speaking in tongues. Evidently some at Corinth tried to perpetuate what was everywhere else understood as an introductory divine corroboration that the message they had just heard, or were hearing, was an authentic message from God. Some Corinthians believers evidently wanted such speaking in tongues to be a regular feature of collective church life. Paul did not forbid the practice, but wrote to them that any such unintelligible speech in church was to be translated so that the whole body of Christ present would benefit. Without an authentic translator, the would-be speaker in tongues was to be silent.

In some of the pagan religions of antiquity, ecstatic speech was a regular feature. Perhaps some of the Corinthian believers knew of such, or had even adhered to such a religion, and wanted to incorporate it into Christianity. Again Paul makes no attempt to argue the point, merely insisting that such be done at home, not as part of corporate worship. Evidently Paul thought that any such genuinely ecstatic speech was rare in Corinth, and so could say that he spoke "in tongues" (ecstatically) more than they.

The next incident involving speaking in tongues again has a distinctly new element. In the first, the new thing had been that the Samaritans, despised by the Jews, but themselves claiming to practice a true Mosaic law religion, had received the gospel as delivered by Philip, though they had spoken in tongues only when Peter and John prayed that they receive the Holy Spirit. Cornelius and his guests were the first God-fearing Gentiles to have the gospel presented to them. With the Corinthians the new feature was the message itself. Now we come to a new class of people, disciples of John the Baptizer. (Acts 19) They had evidently also heard of Jesus as Messiah and accepted him as their Messiah. When Paul asked them if they had received the Holy Spirit they replied that they didn't even know there was a Holy Spirit. The upshot was that Paul evidently baptized them, laid his hands on them (in token of mutual identification of them with himself) upon which they received the Holy Spirit and spoke in tongues.

There was probably another instance of speaking in tongues, though it too is by inference. In Galatians 3:2 Paul introduces a new topic thus: *"Let me ask you only this: Did you receive the Spirit by works of the law, or by hearing with faith?"*

How could Paul write with such assurance that they had received the Spirit? How could he know that they could not deny any such reception of the Spirit? How could he write as if all of them had received the Spirit? He is of course writing to those to whom he personally had brought the gospel. I suggest that the only way Paul could write the way he did is because he was a witness to their reception of the Holy Spirit when they unitedly received his message, and simultaneously and spontaneously spoke in tongues.

To the Philippians and to the Thessalonians Paul says nothing about their receiving the Spirit. He had never been to Rome or to Colossae, and his letter to the Ephesians is evidently a circular letter. So he was not concerned, in writing to the churches in those places about the particulars of the times of their reception of the gospel, and so no mention is made to them of speaking in tongues.

As to his letter to the Galatians, there was more than one church; in each place in which he preached and established a church, there would have been this speaking in tongues on the occasion of their first hearing the gospel.

Neither Luke nor Paul calls particular attention to this mass speaking in tongues. (In 1 Corinthians where Paul writes of speaking in tongues, he specifies that only one individual may do it "in church" at the same time.) In every case recorded or inferred, the speaking was unplanned, spontaneous, and large numbers did it all at once, together. Yet Luke never calls attention to any of these features. He is simply a story teller, giving us the plain, unvarnished facts as he had learned them.

These instances of speaking in tongues are not the kind of thing that a historian would invent. They bear all the marks of authenticity, and give assurance of Luke's trustworthiness. And they are convincing evidence that God truly was working with his servants in the establishment of true Christianity and of the reality of its basic message, "Christ died for our sins."

One point remains. As suggested earlier in passing, the whole exercise of the gift of tongues seems so pointless, apart from the reasons given in the narrative. None of the many other churches Paul established lacked any true benefit in not having experienced speaking in tongues, and those which did, in Corinth and Galatia, were the ones which caused Paul the greatest trouble and concern. What was the point of it all?

The very pointlessness and unreasonableness of tongues is impressive. It seems to be another aspect of God's strange work, alongside his devising an utterly foolish message as the basis of his gospel of pure grace. That grace too is so strange to us, giving the best to reclaim the very worst, and transforming the vile into the pure. And all that without our being able to contribute to it. We are simply not allowed to help. Our part is simply to accept it, gratefully. How very strange! None but God could have thought it up and made it a reality! Thank you, Father.

Comparing the Two Gospels (Differences in Conduct or Behaviour)

The two Gospels contrast in two main respects, visible and invisible.

*   The visible: buildings, altars, animal sacrifices, priests, priestly robes, calendars of holy days, public giving to the temple treasury. Also, the hope of sharing the visible earthly glory of Messiah the King. Temple worship included priests with extensive authority. It was a top-down, rule-dominated system which placed onerous burdens on the faithful. Some of the rules came from the 'law of Moses', others, such as how many steps could be taken on the sabbath, had been added later. This is the realm of organized structures, of formal relationships, of laws written in "stone." This is a system that

requires the exercise of formal authority, enforcement and punishment.

* Invisibly, the people of God are bound together, i.e. the followers of Jesus Christ, into the Body of Christ, the new Israel, the Israel of God (Gal 6:16), the *ekklésia,* brothers and sisters (John 20:17), the family of God (Eph 2:19), the household of faith (Gal 6:10) in which there is no quarrelling or strife (Col 3:13); in which decisions are arrived at by consensus and not by vote (1 Cor 1:10; Phil 2:2; 2 Cor 13:11; Rom 15:5). There is a beautiful example of coming to consensus in the appeal of Paul to Euodia and Syntyche in Philippians 4:2. The appeal is also to others in the congregation to help them agree. This is the realm of personal relationships, which are held together by the kind of love Paul describes in First Corinthians 13. Notice the metaphors here – a body, brothers and sisters, a family, a household.

The invisible: love, compassion, the Holy Spirit, the peace of God, the aim of being Christ-like: compassion, contentment, generosity, patience, peace, self-control, self-giving are evident. The pattern is the self-sacrificial cross of our Lord, Jesus Christ.

The two gospels mirror the tensions in the Old Testament between "the Law" and "the Prophets." Just as the Israelites wished to be "like the nations" and have a king, the Imminent Return Gospel has its equivalent, a Messiah led state. The disciples clearly expected to be in Christ's, the Messiah's cabinet.

Jesus was on the side of the Prophets. He sought to awaken the kingdom in people's hearts by urging them to treat their neighbors respectfully and happily and to love them. By acting in this way consistently they would exhibit the kingdom of God. Jesus' own activities demonstrated what he taught, thus going beyond the letter of the law to its spirit and intention, and so fulfilled it. He showed throughout his life the model of the "great in the kingdom" as the Servant King.

When the cross gospel revelations were given to Paul, he clearly saw, though not immediately or all at one time, their implications for the weekly meeting of the church. These are described above in First Corinthians 11:23-32, and in chapter 14, and amplified in the quotations from Meeks' book *The First Urban Christians.*

Instead of the seeming seditiousness of the first gospel, after Paul had received the revelation that "Christ died for our sins," Paul now could write "Let every person be subject to the governing authorities." (Rom 13:1)

Paul wrote: *"we ourselves boast of you in the churches of God for your steadfastness and faith in all your persecutions and in the afflictions which you are enduring. This is evidence of the righteous judgment of God, that you may be made worthy of the kingdom of God, for which you are suffering - since indeed God deems it just to repay with affliction those who afflict you, and to grant rest with us to you who are afflicted, when the Lord Jesus is revealed from heaven with his mighty angels in flaming fire, inflicting vengeance upon those who do not know God and upon those who do not obey the gospel of our Lord Jesus. They shall suffer the punishment of eternal destruction and exclusion from the presence of the Lord and from the glory of his might, when he comes on that day ... "*(2 Thess 1:4-10)

Two points deserve notice in this passage from the 'imminent return' phase of Paul's ministry. First, God is still thought of in the Old Testament character, violent and vengeful, repaying evil with evil, affliction with affliction. This is in total contrast with his other letter to them as we shall see. Second, Paul says that the believers can "be made worthy of the kingdom of God." That might be possible of a kingdom here on earth, which he was then thinking of, but it contrasts with what he a little later learned.

Within a few months of writing the letter just quoted, Paul wrote the same people, the believers at Thessalonica, another letter (First Thessalonians). In the interval he learned, by revelation, the cross gospel. In it he told them, *"See that none of you repays evil for evil, but always seek to do good to one another and to all."* (1 Thess 5:15)

What Jesus told Peter just before being taken in Gethsemane, about God sending him more than twelve legions of angels, contrasted with "but how then would the scriptures be fulfilled?" To Jesus his cross and resurrection would fulfill the scriptures; to Peter the restoration of David's kingdom would fulfill the scriptures. Peter's was a literal reading, completely misunderstanding the scriptures. Jesus' was a spiritual reading, revealing God's purpose, as does Paul's gospel of the cross.

Current terminology expresses current confusion of trying to combine the two gospels: we see Gospel Tabernacles and Gospel Temples, altars and priests, and holy days in a religious calendar. Christendom has combined Jerusalem and Corinth, with disastrous consequences.

An example of 'imminent return' leadership has already been mentioned in this book: that of Peter's dealing with Ananias and Saphira (Acts 5:1-11). With the judgment of Peter and the death of Ananias and Saphira, *"great fear came upon the whole church, and upon all who heard of these things."* (Acts 5:11) In the 'cross gospel' any dealings with one another should have the result of love, not fear. *"There is no fear in love, but perfect love casts out fear. For fear has to do with punishment, and he who fears is not perfected in love."* (1 John 4:18)

Paul's new gospel of the cross must have raised for him a serious question: What kind of conduct is appropriate for those who are converted through this gospel? It very likely raised another question as well: What is the God really like who is revealed as forgiving people through the death of his Son on the cross?

The first gospel (Imminent Return) is one of self-seeking, self-serving. The true gospel of the cross is self-giving, self-sacrificing. The first is that of "saving one's life;" the second of "losing one's life."

As to daily conduct, Paul wrote: *Let your manner of life be worthy of the gospel of Christ, so that whether I come and see you or am absent, I may hear of you that you stand firm in one spirit, with one mind striving side by side for the faith of the gospel, and not frightened in anything by your opponents. ... So if there is any encouragement in Christ, any incentive of love, any participation in the Spirit, any affection and sympathy, complete my joy by being of the same mind, having the same love, being in full accord and of one mind. Do nothing from selfishness or conceit, but in humility count others better than yourselves. Let each of you look not only to his own interests, but also to the interests of others.* (Phil 1:27-2:4)

Paul progressed still further. Consider what he wrote to the believers in Rome: *"Beloved, never avenge yourselves, but leave it to the wrath of God; for it is written, "Vengeance is mine, I will repay, says the Lord." No, "if your enemy is hungry, feed him; if he is thirsty, give him drink; for by so doing you will heap burning coals upon his head." Do not be overcome by evil, but overcome evil with good"* (Romans 12:19-21). Think too of Galatians 5:22-23 – *"the fruit of the Spirit is love, joy, peace, patience, kindness, goodness, faithfulness, gentleness, self-control."* This latter verse relates not so much to Christian behaviour as to Christian character, the character from which conduct flows.

The four chapters, twelve to fifteen, of Paul's letter to the Romans read like a manual of 'Cross Gospel Conduct.' But then, the bulk of all of his letters, taken as a whole, deal with the behaviour of Christians, in all manner of situations and circumstances. The space in his letters devoted to new teaching for the recipients is comparatively small, and all of it had implications for Christian conduct. And all, written after the letter we call Second Thessalonians, is of conduct to be modeled on Him to whom we are converted, Jesus, who said, *"Come to me, all who labor and are heavy laden, and I will give your rest. Take my yoke upon you, and learn from me; for I am gentle and lowly in heart, and you will find rest for your souls. For my yoke is easy, and my burden is light"*. (Matt 11:28-30)

Robert L. Greenhow

When we examine conduct appropriate to the gospel Paul preached at first, even his advanced law-free gospel, we find a quite different state of affairs. We find even a different view of God, as we have just noted, more like the Old Testament "Jehovah is a Man of War." Violence in which vengeance clothed itself, and condemnation for those "who did not believe the truth" with consequent "punishment of eternal destruction" (2 Thess). Throughout, the gospel of the imminent kingdom seems harsh and uncaring, unfeeling and heedless of the personal conduct of men and women. There is nothing positive in it except the hope of sharing in material prosperity here below. Most people everywhere hope for a more prosperous future, so responding positively to the kingdom gospel did not radically change people's hopes, nor did it change the way they conducted their lives. This is in striking contrast with the Cross Gospel; it changes even the basis on which one's character, hopes and conduct are formed.

A more generalized description of the difference between the two gospels might be what characterizes the two testaments. The Messiah was thought to be a new David, "a man after God's own heart." But David was a man of war, and as such he was kept from building God's temple. Messiah, the new David was also expected to be a man of war, taking vengeance on his enemies, condemning them to destruction. The kingdom gospel really belonged in an Old Testament frame. As such it became outmoded and replaced by the new gospel of Jesus' cross, through which we are reconciled to God (2 Cor 5:19). And our lives are to be characterized by all that characterized Jesus, as we have just noted.

The two different gospels don't admit of mixture, nor does the manner of life appropriate to the one fit the manner of life appropriate to the other. However, what we can't help but see, when we glance at the history of Christendom through the centuries, is confusion and contradiction everywhere, when attempts are made to apply passages of scripture appropriate to one gospel to situations created by the other. Though the gospel of the cross is a gospel of peace, it has often been used as justification for war, as with the Crusades, for which Moslems today upbraid Christians. The executions of the Old Testament are used by Christians today as proper precedent to justify capital punishment. Dare we think of Jesus urging the practice of capital punishment? Many types of violence and vengeance (appropriate to the imminent kingdom gospel) are advocated by Christians who profess to proclaim a cross gospel of forgiveness, love, compassion, generosity, gentleness and peace.

When it is recognized that the New Testament exhibits both kinds of gospel, and that conduct appropriate to each is also shown, we can begin to distinguish between them, and apply scripture passages only to situations envisaged by its appropriate gospel. To rid Christianity of the reproach of being two-faced, or of talking out of both sides of our mouths, we must approach scripture realizing that God has accommodated himself to whatever stage of human development man had reached. The final stage was reached in Jesus, and his gospel is the gospel which Paul proclaimed, the death and resurrection gospel of Jesus, crucified but risen and coming again. And we are to conform our behaviour, not to the world and its standards, but to the standard of our new creation hopes as we realize that we too, in God's eyes, are crucified with Christ, and

143

risen again and glorified with him and even, according to Paul, seated with him in the heavenlies. So as Paul wrote to the Christians at Philippi, *"live your life in a manner worthy of the gospel of Christ."* (Phil 1:27 NRSV)

Jesus had told everyone to repent. His followers were not exempt from the need to repent. To repent in this context is not so much about sins as it is to change one's mind, one's attitude, even one's definitions. The twelve were to change their definition of 'Messiah' and of 'Israel' too. They themselves were the core of the different Israel, the Israel of God, but they didn't recognize that, even though they knew the number 12 was important and saw that their number had to be brought up to that after the defection of Judas. The definition of 'Messiah' too had to lose its earth-bound connotations. The twelve had experienced the truth that they were the Israel of God in a New Age when they cast out demons in the villages of Galilee. That experience should have alerted them to realize that their power, messianic-age power, was not directed *"against flesh and blood but against the principalities, against the powers, against the world rulers of this present darkness."* (Eph 6:12) Jesus as Messiah was to conquer these powers rather than the occupying power of Rome. But all this was beyond the understanding of the twelve.

Because the disciples' thoughts of what Messiah's purpose was, their preaching of the gospel was, of course, according to their ideas. So they preached that Messiah would soon return to re-establish the Davidic kingdom (as their interpretation of the prophets indicated he would). They were by no means exceptional in this; almost all other Jews believed much the same, (and those who didn't believe it knew very well the beliefs of those who did) and understood perfectly what Peter was talking about on the Day of Pentecost. They liked what they heard, after being told that they would not be held accountable for their sin of crucifying their Messiah if they switched sides and truly accepted him as indeed their own long-looked-for Messiah.

All that is written above on behaviour applies to everyone who seeks to follow in the steps of the crucified Lord. But it has particular importance to leaders within the body of Christ, and to the way we "conduct our affairs." Even Paul had to cope with the practical issue of ensuring "order" when significant numbers of believers met together. There was, and there remains, a need to provide teaching to new believers and old. There are practical matters to take care of, so it is a logical step to introduce a measure of organization. And this leads to a group of people who regularly meet, to build up a "usual way of doing things." This becomes a set of traditions. And as these become "institutionalized" and members grow older, there is a danger that these trappings take on a great meaning. There is a danger that "the wrapping, the packaging" becomes the message, and forms of worship suppress the content and true purpose of meeting together.

Just as Old Testament revivals inevitably petered out to formalism and legalism, so the history of the church is replete with revivalist movements that "got out of hand and had to be brought under control" by a hierarchical structure and written doctrines of faith. The fervor of personal relationships often characteristic of the revivalist leaders is slowly transformed into a set of formal statements and relationships between leaders and (registered, formal) members of the church. And so the cross gospel behaviour is in constant danger of being usurped by crown gospel attitudes of centralized control and power. Leaders themselves need to experience the constant renewal of their minds, and guard against this tendency.

Perhaps part of this subtle process of change is due to a reluctance to see that the New Testament writings clearly show these contradictory and competing gospels. We want to believe that the early church was a model of purity, a picture of heaven on earth. We must be forever grateful to Luke who in his always careful and diplomatic way shows us the real story.

How Many Gospels?

My postulate, following Neil, that the earliest gospel was that of the risen Messiah Jesus' imminent return, plus Paul's statements as to other gospels, raises the question as to the content of these other gospels. What is the New Testament evidence for them?

1. Paul's words "If I still preached circumcision (=Judaism) … " (Gal 5.11) refers to his earlier time when he preached the imminent return gospel.
2. Paul's law-free gospel of Messiah's imminent return, developed from the practice he observed at Antioch of converted Jews and converted Gentiles fellowshipping together happily without reference to Jewish customs and observances of the provisions of Moses' law.
3. The Judaizers' gospel of Messiah's imminent return with the stipulation that Gentiles must be circumcised and observe Moses' law.

4.   Paul's gospel of the cross -- "Christ died for our sins." The implications of this apparently were not immediately understood by Paul, beyond "Christ died for us" (1 Thes 5.10).

*   The 'partisan' gospel 'in pretence' which Paul alludes to in Philippians 1.17, was probably similar to #1 or 2 above. Whatever it was it couldn't have been too bad inasmuch as Paul expressed himself as happy that through it Christ was preached.

5.   The other gospel "which is not another", but which Paul twice says was contrary to what he preached to the Galatians, and also a perversion of the gospel of Christ. The probable content of the Galatian Judaizers: not only was Paul's gospel nonsense or madness, but also quite false; that Christ had not died for our sins, that there could have been no purpose in his death inasmuch he died under the divine curse. Nor was there any need for anyone to die for our sins; Jewish ritual sacrifices provided for that. In Paul's view this teaching was so perverse that those who preached it deserved to be cursed.

6.   A gnostic gospel which Paul combated in Colossians, and John in his first letter.

7.   A gospel which Apollos must have preached, since he *"taught accurately the things concerning Jesus, though he knew only the baptism of John."* This gospel could hardly have been any of the above, because *"when Priscilla and Aquila heard him, they took him and expounded to him the way of God more accurately"* (Acts 18:24-26).

Bibliography

Allo, Ernest-Bernard. *Première Épitre aux Corinthiens*. Paris: Gabalda, 1956.

Barclay, William. *The Fourth Gospel and Acts*. Philadelphia: Westminster Press, 1976.
  - *Introduction to the First Three Gospels*. Philadelphia : Westminster Press, 1975

Barrett, Charles Kingsley. *Luke the Historian in Recent Study*. London: Epworth Press, 1961.
  - *Commentary on the First Epistle to the Corinthians*. London: A&C Black,1968.

Barry, Frank Russell. *The Atonement*. Lippincott, 1968.

Beker, Johan Christiaan. *Heirs of Paul: Paul's legacy in the New Testament and in the Church Today*. Minneapolis: Fortress Press, 1991.

Betz, Hans Dieter. *Galatians: a commentary on Paul's letter to the churches in Galatia*. Philadelphia: Fortress Press, 1979.

Bevan, Edwyn. *Christianity*. London: Thornton Butterworth Limited, (1932) fourth impression 1935.

Blackman, EC. *Biblical Inspiration*. p 72.

Blunt, John James. *Undesigned Coincidences in the Writings both of the Old and New Testaments: an argument of their veracity: with an appendix containing undesigned coincidences between the Gospels, and Acts, and Josephus*. New York: R. Carter, 1851.

Bruce, Frederick Fyvie. *New Testament History*. Garden City, NY: Doubleday, 1980.
  - *Paul: Apostle of the Free Spirit*. Exeter UK: Paternoster, 1977.

Bultmann, Rudolf. *Jesus and the Word*. Translated by L Smith and E Lantero. London: Charles Scribner's Sons, 1958. (© 1934)

Caird, George B. *The Apostolic Age*. London: Duckworth, 1955 reprinted 1974.
  - *Saint Luke*. (Pelican Gospel Commentaries edited by DE Nineham) London: Penguin Books, 1963 .

Collingwood, Robin George. *The Idea of History: With Lectures 1926-1928*. Edited by Jan van der Dussen. UK: Oxford University Press, 1946.

Conzelmann, Hans. *History of Primitive Christianity*. Abingdon Press, 1973

Dahl, Nils Alstrup. *The Crucified Messiah*. Minneapolis: Augsburg Publishing House, 1974.

Davies, William David. *Paul and Rabbinic Judaism*. London: SPCK, 1948.

Deluz, Gaston. *La Sagesse de Dieu; Explication de la 1re Epitre aux Corinthiens* Neuchatel: Delachaux & Niestle, 1959.

Denney, James. *The Christian Doctrine of Reconciliation*. New York: George H. Doran Co., 1918.
- *The Death of Christ*. London: Hodder and Stoughton, 1902. edited by RVG Tasker and reprinted London: Tyndale Press, 1952.

De Rosa, Peter. *Christ and Original Sin*. London: Geoffrey Chapman, 1967.

Dillistone, Frederick William. *The Significance of the Cross*. Philadelphia: Westminster Press, 1944.

Dodd, Charles Harold. *The Apostolic Preaching The and its Developments: Three Lectures with an Eschatology and History*. London: Hodder and Stoughton, 1936.

Douglas, James Dixon. Editor. *New Bible Dictionary*. Grand Rapids, Michigan: Eerdmans, 1962.

Dunn, James Douglas Grant. *Unity and diversity in the New Testament: an inquiry into the character of earliest Christianity*. London: SCM Press, 1977.

Edrick. "The 3 Temptations of Jesus." The 3 Temptations of Jesus. The Epistle, 2009. Web. 07 Mar. 2013. epistle.us/articles/jesustemptation.html.

Ellis, E. E. quoting F C Baur in his article "Paul" in the *New Bible Dictionary*. Douglas, James Dixon. editor. Grand Rapids, Michigan: Eerdmans, 1962.

Fee, Gordon. *Paul, the Spirit, and the People of God*. Grand Rapids, Michigan: Baker Publishing Group, 1994. Reprint 1996.

Filson, Floyd Vivian. *The New Testament Against its Environment: the Gospel of Christ, the Risen Lord*. London: SCM, 1950.
  - *Three Crucial Decades: Studies in the Book of Acts*. Richmond, Virginia: John Knox Press, 1963.
  - "The Journey Motif in Luke-Acts" in Gasque & Martin, eds, *Apostolic History and the Gospel* Grand Rapids, Michigan: Eerdmans, 1970.

Frend, William Hugh Clifford. *The Early Church*. London: Hodder and Stoughton, 1965.

Foakes-Jackson, FJ. *The History of the Christian Church from the Earliest Times to A.D. 461*. 6th edition Cambridge: J. Hall & Son, 1891.

Gasque W. Ward and Ralph P. Martin. Editors. *Apostolic History and the Gospel* Grand Rapids, Michigan: Eerdmans, 1970.

Glatzer, Nahum. Foreword to *The Pharisees*, by R Travers Herford. Boston: Beacon Press, 1962.

Godet, Frederic Louis. *A Commentary on the Gospel of Luke*. Edinburgh: T & T Clark, 1879.

Goppelt, Leonard. *Apostolic and Post-Apostolic Times*. New York: Harper Torchbooks, 1970.

Goguel, Maurice. *The Birth of Christianity. (La Naissance du Christianisme Paris: Payot, 1946.)*. London: Allen & Unwin, 1953.

Goodspeed, Edgar J. *A Life of Jesus*. New York: Harper & Brothers, 1950.

Guignebert, Charles. *The Jewish World in the Time of Jesus*. New York: University Books 1959.

Haenchen, Ernst. *Acts of the Apostles*. Philadelphia: Westminster Press, 1971.

Hengel, Martin. *The Atonement: a Study of the Origins of the Doctrine in the New Testament*. London: SCM, 1981.
- *The Pre-Christian Paul*. Philadelphia: Trinity Press International, 1991.
- *Acts & the History of Earliest Christianity*. London, SCM Press, 1979.

Héring, J. *The First Epistle of Saint Paul to the Corinthians*. London: Epworth Press, 1962.

Hodge, Charles. *An Exposition of the First Epistle to the Corinthians*, New York: R. Carter, 1857. Grand Rapids, Michigan: Eerdmans, 1980.

Hoskyns, Edwyn Clement, and Francis Noel Davey. *The Fourth Gospel*. (1940) London: Faber and Faber, 1947.

Howard, George. *Paul: Crisis in Galatia A study in Early Christian Theology.* New York: Cambridge University Press, 1979.

Ironside, Henry Allen. *Lectures on the Book of Acts.* New York: Loizeaux Bros., 1943.

Johnson, Paul. *A History of Christianity.* New York: Atheneum, 1976.

Juel, Donald. *Luke–Acts: The Promise of History.* Atlanta: John Knox Press, 1983.

Klausner, Joseph. *The Messianic Idea in Israel.* Translated by W. F. Stinespring. London: G Allen and Unwin, 1954.

Ladd, GE. "Revelation and Tradition in Paul", In *Apostolic History & the Gospel*, Edited by Gasque, W. Ward and Ralph P Martin. Grand Rapids, Michigan: Eerdmans, 1970.

Lake, Kirsopp. *Landmarks in the History of Early Christianity.* London: Macmillan, 1920.

Lampe, Geoffrey William Hugo. *Luke & the Church of Jerusalem.* London: Athlone Press, 1969.

Longenecker, Richard. *Paul, Apostle of Liberty.* New York: Harper and Row, 1964.
  - *NT Social Ethics for Today.* Grand Rapids, Michigan: Eerdmans, 1984.

Macintosh, Hugh Ross. *The Christian Experience of Forgiveness.* London: Nisbet & Co., 1927.

Manschreck, Clyde Leonard. *History of Christianity in the World*. Englewood Cliffs, New Jersey: Prentice-Hall, 1985.

Manson, Thomas Walter. *Ministry and Priesthood, Christ's and Ours*. London: The Epworth Press, 1958.
- *The Teaching of Jesus*. Cambridge: Cambridge University Press, 1931.
- *The Servant-Messiah*. Cambridge: Cambridge University Press, 1961.
- *Ethics and the Gospel*. Cambridge: Cambridge University Press, 1960.
- *Studies in the Gospels and Epistles*. Philadelphia: Westminster Press, 1962.

Martin, Ralph P. *The Epistle of Paul to the Philippians*. London: Tyndale Press, 1959.

Meeks, Wayne A. *The First Urban Christians, The Social World of the Apostle Paul*. New Haven: Yale University Press, 1983.

Morris, Leon. *The First Epistle of Paul to the Corinthians, An Introduction and Commentary (Tyndale New Testament Commentaries)*. Grand Rapids, MI: Eerdmans, (1958) 1979.

Neil, William. *Letter of Paul to the Galatians*. Cambridge: Cambridge University Press, 1967.

Neusner, Jacob. *From Politics to Piety. The Emergence of Pharisaic Judaism*. Englewood Cliffs: Prentice-Hall, 1973.

Ramm, Bernard. *Special Revelation and the Word of God.* Grand Rapids, Michigan: Eerdmans, 1961.

Robinson, John AT. *In the End God.* London: Collins, Fontana Books, 1968.
- *Redating the New Testament.* London: SCM Press, 1976.
- *Jesus and His Coming.* London: SCM Press, 1957.

Robinson, Henry. Wheeler, *Redemption and Revelation.* New York and London: Harper & Bros., 1942.

Ruef, John. *Paul's First Letter to Corinth.* Philadelphia: Westminster Press, 1977.

Sandmel, Samuel. *Judaism and Christian Beginnings.* New York: Oxford University Press, 1978.

Scott, Charles Archibald Anderson. *Christianity According to Paul.* London: Cambridge University Press, 1927.
- *St Paul: The Man and the Teacher.* Cambridge: Cambridge University Press, 1936.
- *Foot-Notes to St Paul.* Cambridge: Cambridge University Press, 1935.

Segal, Alan F. *Rebecca's Children, Judaism and Christianity in the Roman World.* Cambridge, MA: Harvard University Press, 1986.

Simon, Marcel. *Jewish Sects at the Time of Jesus.* Translated by James H. Farley. Philadelphia: Fortress Press, 1967.

Stagg, Frank. *The Book of Acts, The Early Struggle for an Unhindered Gospel.* Nashville: Broadman Press, 1955.

Stewart, James. *A Man in Christ: The Vital Elements of St. Paul's Religion*. London: Hodder and Stoughton Limited, 1935.

Taylor, Vincent. *Jesus and his Sacrifice*. London: Macmillan, 1937.

Wernle, Paul. *Beginnings of Christianity*. Edited by Wm D Morrison. London: Williams and Norgate; New York: Putnam, 1903.

Westcott, Brooke Foss. *Epistle to Hebrews*. London: Macmillan, 1889 (1952, liv).

Whale, John S. *Christian Doctrine: Eight Lectures Delivered in the University of Cambridge to Undergraduates of All Faculties*. Cambridge: Cambridge University Press, 1952.

Wilkinson, John Thomas, *Principles of Biblical Interpretation*. London: Epworth, 1960.

Young, Frances Margaret. *Sacrifice and the Death of Christ*. London: SCM Press, 1975.

Zeitlin, Irving M. *Jesus and the Judaism of his Time*. Cambridge, UK: Polity Press 1988.